WHAT DO WOMEN WANT

"Backed up by their experiences with hundreds of women and men in therapy over the past 10 years, these two psychotherapists cut right to the heart of the matter. Every sentence, every anecdote hits home. . . . Any woman who reads this book will recognize herself, her friends, her loves. This should be compulsory reading . . ."
—*St. Petersburg Times*

". . . the old bargain (he depends on her for nurturance, she depends on him for economic support and sexual legitimacy) has been shattered. Women want more than a man who makes a good living: they want a man who provides warmth and commitment."
—*Vogue*

". . . a well-thought-out analysis of the nature of women's dependency needs."
—*Publishers Weekly*

". . . Excellent . . . The founders of women's therapy centers in New York and London are well qualified to address Freud's classic question. Highly recommended."
—*Library Journal*

Also by Susie Orbach

FAT IS A FEMINIST ISSUE
FAT IS A FEMINIST ISSUE II
UNDERSTANDING WOMEN:
A FEMINIST PSYCHOANALYTIC APPROACH
(with Luise Eichenbaum)
WHAT DO WOMEN WANT
(with Luise Eichenbaum)

EXPLODING THE MYTH OF DEPENDENCY

Luise Eichenbaum & Susie Orbach

BERKLEY BOOKS, NEW YORK

WHAT DO WOMEN WANT

A Berkley Book / published by arrangement with
Coward-McCann, Inc.

PRINTING HISTORY
Coward-McCann edition / May 1983
Berkley edition / May 1984

ISBN: 0-425-06770-X

A BERKLEY BOOK ® TM 757,375
Berkley Books are published by The Berkley Publishing Group,
200 Madison Avenue, New York, New York 10016.
The name "BERKLEY" and the stylized "B" with design
are trademarks belonging to Berkley Publishing Corporation.
PRINTED IN THE UNITED STATES OF AMERICA

This book is dedicated to
Jeremy Pikser and Joseph Schwartz

CONTENTS

WHAT
DO
WOMEN
WANT

PREFACE

❖ ❖ ❖

We opened the doors to The Women's Therapy Centre in London on April 8, 1976, offering psychotherapy and counseling services to women and their families. This was the first project of its kind and scope in Great Britain and we were soon overwhelmed by the response to our facilities by women from all over the country who came for counseling. Women talked about the emotional upsets that pervaded their lives—their marriages, being single, difficulties they experienced in their jobs, the texture of parenting, the meshing of role expectations and changing opportunities for women. In the last six years thousands of women, young, middle-aged, and old, have come to the Centre and shared with us what was on their minds and in their hearts. As the Centre grew we traveled around England. There was great interest from mental health institutions, women's studies programs, and women's groups about the work of The Women's Therapy Centre.

In women's therapy groups and theme-centered workshops women learned to value their own experiences and to rethink aspects of their lives and their emo-

1

tional yearnings. Barriers that existed among women from different class backgrounds, life-styles, occupational groups, ages, and even sexual orientation dissolved as women discovered together the commonality of their emotional and psychological experiences. Underneath the seemingly vast differences in how each individual woman lived her life were themes, directions, conflicts, and anxieties shared by other women in the group. Hearing about them from one another, women could identify what was troubling them and get support and encouragement for the changes they wanted to make.

In revealing themselves and their concerns, the women who attended the Centre shaped its growth and direction. Programs we developed as therapists were propelled by the desires and the anguish we discerned in the lives of the women we were meeting. At the very heart of many women's concerns and confusions was the theme of dependency. In order to understand more about this theme we thought about our own experiences and about the experiences of our clients in long-term individual therapy. We examined how this issue came up in groups, we looked at what happened between couples and in friendships, and we began to design workshops that focused directly on the theme.

In the early days of the women's liberation movement links began to be made between the economic conditions of women's lives and their emotional consequences. Women in our culture were brought up to be economically dependent on men. We all knew of the bargain to be made in marriage—women would look after house, home and children; men would make sure the bills and expenses were met. Many women stayed in unsatisfactory marriages because there were few alternatives. Even today many women and men who would prefer to live separately continue living together because economic conditions are structured with so few, and increasingly dwindling, alternatives. One of the first issues the women's liberation movement took up was the issue of women's second-class economic status. Many women have become self-supporting but the battle has yet to be won. Women still earn much less than men in the same occupational sphere, women are still the last to be hired and the first to be fired. The economic structure does indeed relate to the emotional sphere but not in an easy mechanistic way.

Many women we encountered had achieved economic independence and they used this independence to reduce their reliance on men. They still sought close relationships but did not allow themselves to feel their dependencies in these relationships. A new notion circulated in the women's movement. Relationships in which women felt vulnerable because they were emotionally dependent came to be judged as old-fashioned, not very feminist, too caught up with ideas of romance and ownership of the other, and so on. Women were eager to denounce their dependent parts and experience the relief of not being overwhelmed by the cloying intensity and the drama that were so often part and parcel of an intimate relationship. Many women felt freed by not being in close relationships and not worrying, feeling insecure so much of the time. Women began to see how intimate relationships often produced dreadful feelings of insecurity rather than the harmony and safe place that close contact with another had seemed to hold out at first. Women sought to be economically independent so that their emotional relationships could take on a different shape.

Our work both at The Women's Therapy Centre and in New York led us to see that the solution to women's "problems" with dependency was not all that simple. It wasn't that women who could not support themselves were successfully negotiating relationships that didn't stir up terrific longings for contact, emotional interdependence, and nurturance. Women, whether self-supporting or not, disclosed continuing confusion about the topic of emotional dependency, which pointed out that the relationship between the economic and the psychological spheres was more complicated than might have first appeared. That is, women involved in relationships with men found that although they had made enormous changes, their men had not. Women's developing autonomy clearly forced certain issues out into the open for couples. Men were making behavioral adjustments to women's demands, but changes in couple relationships clearly required more than men doing the dishes and helping out with the kids. The psychological terrain of the relationship between men and women had not yet been mapped. In effect, men were being excluded, as well as being let off the hook, from making deep personal and political changes. For us the women's movement had offered another strand. It meant the growth, and not the constriction, of the emotional side of relationships. Emotional relationships were valued. We relied on friends and lovers, and we recognized that dependency. We began to see that dependency was a problem for both men and women. We didn't want to be in retreat from dependency, for we knew how very important friendships and love relationships already were in our lives and that these relationships could give us support for growth and autonomous development.

We were eager to understand how to look at the yearnings that women felt rather than to reject them, and we asked ourselves how men managed their dependency needs.

As psychotherapists we knew that attitudes we hold are intricately linked to emotional issues that are not terribly obvious at first glance. We knew that if we could look behind the words *dependency, love, nurturance, wanting,* and *insecurity,* we might be able to understand something central about women's (and men's) experiences. In our practice we continually heard of our clients' insecurities, expressed through jealousy, competition, envy or mistrust of others. Inside of each woman was a part of herself that was isolated, hidden, that felt abandoned, rejected, and infantile. We had to ask ourselves, if society directs women to be dependent why do they feel so insecure about others being there for them; if it's okay for women to be dependent why does it take months in therapy for a woman client to let us see the dependent part of herself? Over the past decade on both sides of the ocean this theme of dependency seemed to be at the very core of women's psychology.

The embryo of the theme of dependency began to emerge early in our clinical work. In those years we discussed our findings that women had a great deal of difficulty in receiving attention in the therapy relationship. Being listened to, taken seriously, and related to with empathy and care was obviously an unfamiliar position for a woman to be in. We noticed that a client would make attempts to reciprocate the care and attention of the therapist. That after three or four sessions she would feel that perhaps she had had enough of what she was needing. We began to see that client after client experienced discomfort in digesting the possibility that we genuinely were interested in what she had to say and who she was. She found it equally problematic to believe that our care and concern were authentic. It was becoming clear that women could listen to others, give attention to others, be on the giving side of a relationship with an ease that she could not come near when on the receiving end. In short, we saw and experienced that women strongly protected against showing their dependency needs. Women expressed feelings of shame and self-dislike for having these needs in the first place. Time and again we heard our women clients assuming that they should not and could not expect care and attention from anyone else; that they should be able to take care of themselves; that needing equaled weakness and childishness. At the same time they spoke of their assumptions that they had to be available to respond to the needs of others. The imbalance was glaring. This need to give and the difficulty with receiving was such a feature of each woman we encountered that we began to see it as central to the development of women's psychology. When we shared our observations of this phenomenon with women in groups they sighed with recognition and the realization that this was not just a personal issue but one that touched us all. As theme after theme began to be unraveled in women's psychology women saw themselves in one another and felt both relief and closeness with one another. The various barriers that had divided women's experiences seemed to disappear as mothers, daughters, grandmothers, teenagers, middle-class women, working-class women, lesbians, and heterosexual women felt one another's pain to be so like their own. We are continually struck by how emotionally similar women's lives are regardless of individual life situations. Our views on the theme of dependency are continually confirmed by the many women we talk to and see clinically.

In this book we have tried to include the experiences of all of the women we have worked with. This means that you will meet women of different ages: some of them married, some single, some living with other women. Their openness enabled us to assemble the kaleidoscope of experiences that make up the many facets of dependency we present here. We gratefully appreciate what we have learned from our clients and hope that our current understanding of women's and men's psychology, its interplay and consequences for couple relationships and women's friendships, will resonate for you. The authors would like to thank Linda Healey for her thoughtful editorial help.

—*Luise Eichenbaum*
Susie Orbach
1982

INTRODUCTION

Exploding the Myth
of Dependency

It is now over fifty years since Freud threw up his hands
in exasperation over the question of women's inner
lives. What do women want? Since then psychoanalysts,
humanists, researchers of human relationships and, of
course, women and men also have pondered this question. Defined by others and so often living in their
shadow, women themselves have only recently articu-
lated their desires, their wants, and their most intimate
thoughts. Men, meanwhile, have been perplexed by
women's demands. Because men's and women's socialization and daily life experience are very different, it
often feels like women live in one emotional world and
men in another. The separateness of these worlds can
cause ravaging consequences when the emotional lives
of women and men meet in intimate relationships. At
present we are witnessing a crisis in male-female relationships. But what makes women and men tick is not
really so different. In this book we will show that what
makes it so hard for them to relate satisfactorily is a
deep confusion and misunderstanding of the dependency needs of themselves and each other.

The thread of dependency runs through all human relationships. Modern marriage is a complex web of dependency, sexuality, and autonomy. For too long we have labored under the myth that men are big and strong and independent; that women are passive, helpless, and dependent. And yet, the attempts of the women's liberation movement to break these stereotypes have all too often floundered on the limitations that women, themselves, feel are a part of their emotional makeup. Why?

In this book we begin to answer this question by proposing a radically new way to view women's and men's emotional dependency. It emerges from our clinical practice as psychotherapists in which we investigated the intimate thoughts and feelings of hundreds of clients—women and couples—and discovered time and again the similar emotional dynamics of couples. In love affairs, marriages, and intimate relationships with men women discussed how they sought, but rarely could sustain, the emotional connection they longed for. Moreover, in their disappointments in love they were forced to confront another, often previously obscure, aspect of their personalities. They found that their emotional lives had become overwhelmingly wrapped up in a search for contact and understanding from their mates. They had begun to be people who showed dependent, "clingy" behavior. Men, meanwhile, felt frustrated, bewildered, and confused about what their partners wanted. What do women want?

Colette Dowling's *Cinderella Complex* (1981) has struck a resounding chord in today's women because, for perhaps the first time, this crucial issue of dependency has been brought into the open. However, while her case studies are accurate, she lacks the psychoanalytic or clinical understanding to draw the correct conclusions. Her thesis, that progress toward equality of the sexes is hampered by a learned dependency that goes with growing up female, misses, from our perspective, the central point at issue.

Dependency is not, as Ms. Dowling suggests, "the refusal to accept responsibility." It is a basic human need. Psychological development theorists and psychotherapeutic practitioners know that achieving autonomy and independence rests on the *gratification* of dependency needs. It is only when a child feels confident that she or he *can* depend on others that the child grows up feeling confident enough to be independent. Women are indeed fearful of independence and success. But this is not because they have been raised to depend on others. It is precisely for the opposite reason: Women are raised to be depended *upon*; to place their emotional needs second to those of others. While women have traditionally been dependent economically, they have always been the emotional caretakers of the family. At the same time that women are depended upon for emotional support and nurturance, they learn to *behave* dependently. Girls learn from very early on that it is dependent behavior (passivity, helplessness, submissiveness) that will get them what they are searching for—someone to consistently care for them. However, it is important to distinguish between the ways in which women behave dependently ("I can't screw this screw into the wall") and women's true emotional dependency needs ("I need someone who will understand me and love me").

In confusing economic dependence and emotional dependency, Colette Dowling assumes that, firstly, women's emotional dependency needs are satisfactorily met. This does not match with our own clinical findings, for if these needs are met why do women continue to have such complicated feelings about them? Secondly, Colette Dowling suggests that women should be more like men, without taking into account the ways in which, in an unacknowledged way, men rely on women. She does not address the fact that men's emotional dependency needs are, in fact, more consistently catered to than women's and that this fact has a direct correlation to men's ability to be more "independent." Dowling tends to confirm what most women feel and fear, that is, that their dependency needs signify weakness. Our account offers a deeper analysis of this phenomenon.

Over the past twelve years many thousands of women attempted to tackle dependency in their efforts toward women's liberation. Women know that dependency is a critical theme in their day-to-day lives—it is woven into the very fabric of their experience of what it means to be a woman. It is only recently that we are coming to understand that liberation does not mean an "independence" of emotional isolation, of not needing from others. We must throw off the dependent behavior traits and stereotypes that cripple us, but ultimately this will only be possible when women receive gratification of the very human needs of human interdependency. This means that men as well as women have an enormous task in front of them.

In our culture both men and women come to feel ashamed of dependency feelings. It seems to signify weakness in both sexes but in different ways. Boys grow up on one side of an unbalanced coin. Their dependency needs are hidden from view, but more successfully answered. A boy grows up learning to depend on women, first his mother and then his wife. A girl grows up learning she will have to give up her mother without getting wifely love in her place. Paradoxically, precisely because there is a continuity in the responding to male dependency needs, those very needs are less exposed. Both women and men cooperate in this process of keeping from view men's dependency needs. The true dialogue of women's and men's dependency on each other is not acknowledged.

From infancy to adulthood we depend on one another for our growth and well-being. Society is an intricate network of dependency relationships, both economic and emotional. A superficial observation of ourselves as adults would seem to show that men do what they were brought up to do. By and large they marry, give economic support to their wives and children, at the same time as they stand on their own, somewhat separate from the family, concerned with work and outside interests. Women, for their part, marry, have babies, look after and are absorbed by the emotional and domestic needs of the family (whether or not they work outside the home). This is the exchange we are all promised in marriage, and even though there has been a tremendous upheaval in family life in the last decade, the written and unwritten rules of this very crude sketch affect our sense of ourselves, our obligations, and our expectations in our intimate relationships.

The roles that women and men take up are so very different, and the psychological roads we must travel in growing up reflect this. We are all aware of how, in obvious ways, sex-role stereotyping has affected us and influences how we rear our children. Girls are supposed to be sweet and demure, boys are supposed to be active and brave. What we might be less clear about is how our deeply personal concerns, anxieties, and insecurities are also a reflection of this same phenomenon. How we relate to the great themes of love, hate, desire, self-expression, closeness, and separateness, and how we experience our disappointments, our pleasures, our needs and hopes being met or not met, or our entitlement to our desires, mirror what we have experienced in our early development about these emotional states. In other words, boys and girls are, if you like, motivated in subtly different ways emotionally.

Our relationships are guided from the first day of our lives by our parents', close relatives', and teachers' conscious and unconscious sense of their own and our gender. Gender permeates the deepest reaches of ourselves. The most central aspects of our personality development are shaped by whether we are girls or boys. That is not to say that deep down women and men have such different emotional lives, but rather that our emotional and inner experiences are honed in gender-related ways. We grow up with the idea that men must be and are independent, strong, able, and competent. A man who feels himself to be lacking essential masculine attributes can come to feel inadequate and uncomfortable in himself. A woman, we learn, must be nurturing, connected to others, and attractive. A woman who doesn't see herself this way can feel like a freak.

When we look deep into women's and men's psyches to see what really makes up a woman and what makes up a man, we find emotional states that are dramatically different from the gendered role patterns that appear on the surface. Men are brought up to display their independence and separateness. But we discover, in fact, that men are quite hesitant, even afraid, to disclose that they feel emotionally dependent. They will often resist such an idea or retreat from an examination of their dependency needs with a vehemence. This discomfort with the theme of dependency at a deeper level tells us something, for a basic protective psychological mechanism is at work. One develops a defensive stance when one fears (unconsciously) a threat to one's conception of self, the loss of something felt as important, or as a protection against a painful or unpleasant idea. When men shy away from exploring the issue of dependency in their own lives, they may be trying to cover up or not disturb the rather precarious view instilled in them in relation to this theme, which does not meet, at a deep level, their emotional experience. But behind the display lives another self: a self who is vulnerable, dependent, and capable of being deeply hurt; a self who counts on a woman—be it mother, lover, wife, or girlfriend—to be there for him, to relate to him, to be concerned with his emotional well-being, to lean on and rely on for a certain kind of emotional caretaking and nurturance.

All of us are utterly dependent in infancy. In the course of our development we become more and more physically adept while our personalities form and take shape in the context of the various relationships we make in our families. The little boy starts off life dependent on his mother, who will often be his sole caretaker. If he goes to daycare or is looked after by other family members, his guardians will doubtless be female. A boy comes to know dependency in relation to women. It is women who have the power to comfort him or, as he may perceive it at times, withhold this capacity from him. From the arms of mother, sister, aunt, or grandmother the boy leaves home to another environment shaped by a woman, the kindergarten or nursery school, and to another woman, the female teacher. The authority figure, the nurturing person, the central persons in his world are female. As the boy grows up, he and those around him anticipate a future for him that will always involve a close relationship with a woman. Eventually he will be able to bring his emotional life and his dependency needs into a marriage. *In a sense we could say that his needs for emotional nurturance are addressed without him having to especially confront them or spell them out.* This is the background against which he hears the various injunctions and rules about masculinity. His fathers, peers, teachers, and the women around him introduce him to the elements of sex-role stereotyping of what it means to be a man: hiding his emotions, keeping up a good front, developing confidence, projecting independent and courageous attributes. Hidden from view then, and presented even in their opposite form, as we shall see, are men's dependency needs. Every woman knows that men rely on them and count on them and that the equation of men being independent and women dependent is a false one.

A girl grows up knowing that she will bring children into the world who will depend on her, and that she will be connected to a husband for whom she will provide nurturance, caring, and an emotional environment. Just like the little boy, the little girl's personality develops in a predominantly female ambiance. She, like her brother, depends first on mother and then other women for her emotional and physical growth. But the girl's journey in adult life takes a dramatic shift, because women do not marry women (who are taught to nurture). They marry men, who have rarely had a chance to develop the nurturing aspects of their personalities. In tune with sex-role stereotyping imposed on females, girls grow up learning to be sweet, kind, a bit helpless and accepting. They learn to modify or squash their impulses toward independence and self-expression.

Within the constellation of reactions a girl comes to know as hers, she develops tentative and clingy behaviors. She *appears* dependent, incompetent, and somewhat fragile. She learns to look outside of herself for guidance and leadership. But behind this person lives a person who, whatever her inner state, deals with the emotional underpinnings of her various family relationships, a person who knows that others rely on and lean on her, a person who fears that she will never really be able to depend on others or never feels all right about her dependency.

These sex-role personalities and behaviors that women and men develop in order to be at home in the world extract the tremendous emotional cost of depriving all of us of feeling good, safe, and expansive inside of ourselves. The patriarchal system shapes our sense of gender, and consequently who we feel we are, in damaging ways. How women relate with men, how men relate with women, and women relate with one another reveal extraordinarily complicated patterns of dependency needs that are hidden, distorted, and rarely talked about or met straightforwardly. In our work as psychotherapists, seeing women on their own and heterosexual couples, we have come to the startling conclusion that while girls and women are raised to display dependent behavior—which is in reality more of a deference behavior, a looking up to the man—they are cautioned against showing their real emotional dependency needs. *Girls learn early that in the most profound sense they must rely on themselves, there is no one to take care of them emotionally*. They *cannot* assume—as does the man— that there will be someone for them to bring their emotional lives to.

The ability to depend on others is crucial to growth and development. A child needs to feel that he or she can depend on the adults he or she is close to. For it is only when a child feels confident that he or she *can* depend on others that the child can develop with the security and confidence that allows one to become independent. A male or female child who grows up with this kind of experience can more easily look forward to life outside the family with excitement, with the expectation of fitting in, of looking to new experiences with confidence that they will be enriching. A child who has been sufficiently nurtured, who knows that she or he is loved for herself or himself, who can depend on her or his parents for genuine support approaches life in the spirit of interchange and interdependence. Such a child will find the world full of inviting and satisfying relationships and projects. A child who has not had this kind of introduction to life will feel more insecure and on some level will always be searching for the contact she or he missed and now craves. The world will appear more complex. It is a potentially embracing environment, but the bridge to it may be paved with fear, disappointment, and despair.

In our society too few people receive the kind of nurturance that allows them to anticipate relationships with joy. Our early relationships can be fraught with disappointment and misunderstanding. Many of us live with a missing piece inside, a confusion and worry; we yearn for a soul mate who will love us, understand us and help us to face ourselves. Many of us have a needy part that is hidden away from the world and from ourselves.

But as we shall see, the shape and texture of men's and women's needy parts, their sense of emotional connection, reflect the differences in gender role upbringing.

The need for nurturance and emotional dependency stays with us throughout life. When we are understood and responded to we feel more whole within ourselves and with the world. Emotional connection sustains us just like the meals we eat and the air we breathe. It is a vital food that nourishes and regenerates our psyches. Without it we suffer privation and the limiting of our emotional life.

The stark reality of the unequal exchange between women's and men's dependency needs is something that we are just beginning to see and are trying to understand more clearly, because the patterns of heterosexual relating we grew up with are changing. Our society is engaged in a huge social transformation in how the sexes relate to each other and to themselves. Only ten years ago women were having babies early in their twenties, as they had been for decades. Women worked outside the home in some capacity but saw their central identity as linked to their family. Today many more women work outside the home, many heads of households are female, women are marrying later and postponing having children.

These are dramatic changes to have occurred in such a short space of time. They have touched all of our lives, directly or indirectly. We all know women and men who are choosing to live on their own; we all know families in which heterosexuality is not the only sexual orientation for all members; we all know women who have chosen not to have children; and we all know women who are now able to support themselves economically. At the same time that options for women have been expanding, men's traditional role in the family has been threatened. Men are being dislodged from their position as the primary breadwinners[1] both by the worsening economic situation and by women's changing role. Consequently, what women and men do bring to marriage and intimate relationships and what they look for in them can be expected to have changed equally dramatically. In fact, while women may not look to men to support them economically or to provide them with legitimacy for being sexual, and while men may not automatically assume fatherhood, many aspects of what we seek in a love partner are changing very slowly. The changes in all of us at a private and emotional level have not kept pace with the broad changes in family arrangements. The societal changes are allowing us to peek behind the veil of marriage to the political nature of the transactions and psychodynamics in our intimate rela-

[1] This has been an economic fiction for a long time but a believed state of affairs.

tionships. Now that so many more women are sharing the economic costs of raising a family, certain emotional transactions that were not obvious before have become dramatically apparent. It is as though the overwhelming need for a husband to provide economic support and sexual legitimacy screened out the flaws and discrepancies in the emotional exchanges between a husband and wife. Now that this veil is disintegrating, the dissatisfactions in intimate relationships are emerging. Ruth no longer stays with Harry because, despite the lack of intimacy, closeness, and feelings of friendship, "he's a good man, I never had to ask for anything materially." Ruth feels frustrated, cheated and aggrieved. Harry, who has given what he knows how to give—a nice house, steady participation in the community, hard work to provide a good standard of living—is perplexed. "What *does* she want?" This book was written to address this question and to enable us to understand these dynamics in intimate relationships so that we can transform our relationships to better meet our needs.

In this book we are at once writing about what is and arguing for what could be. We interweave theory with the stories of women and men we have met in the course of our work as psychotherapists. We are describing the lives of individual women and men but the issues that affect them apply to women and men across class and ethnic backgrounds. We are examining the impact of child-rearing arrangements where by and large mothers raise children, at the same time we plead for an urgent restructuring of familial domestic arrangements. We concentrate on the mother-daughter and mother-son relationship, for it is primarily women who raise children, but we argue (in chapter VIII) for the involvement of men in the care of children from infancy on. We are describing the structure of relating in mostly heterosexual relationships, because we have all experienced the pressure to have our sexuality conform to our societal arrangements, but we passionately believe in a freer sexuality that allows for love between women and women, men and men, and men and women. What we describe in these pages are painful themes that arise, we believe, as a result of our gendered arrangements. We hope that the reader, in seeing herself or himself on the page, will recognize how deeply gender shapes her or his emotional life and the ways in which we relate. We hope that the struggles of the women and men we describe provide both a sense of optimism and one of urgency about the need to address these issues in order for us to relate more fully.

I

❖ ❖ ❖

Forbidden Feelings:
Women and Dependency

"All I want is to know that someone is *really* there for
me; then I know I could relax and go off and do my own
thing."

Helen is twenty-seven, a bookkeeper and unmarried.
She used to live with Bob but they broke up two years
ago. Since then she has dated a lot of men. We see her
now getting ready to go out on her first real date with
Paul, a thirty-five-year-old divorced social worker
whom she met a week before on a blind date. It is Saturday evening and Helen is lounging in her bath, steaming
her face before the big event. The afternoon was spent
at Macy's buying new shoes, a belt, and a scarf to complete tonight's outfit. She's been so excited by the date,
she's hardly eaten all day. She is savoring the possibility
that they will "fall in love" and have a wonderful time
together. Already she has fantasies of meeting his
parents, of introducing him to hers, of the summer
vacation filled with daiquiris and piña coladas and him
at Fire Island. . . . Six months later Paul and Helen are

seeing each other regularly. Their relationship has already lost its glitter. Helen is frustrated and disappointed and she is worried about how Paul spends the evenings that they are apart. She gets very clingy and feels things would be much better if they lived together. She has become particularly jealous of Renata, a work mate of Paul's, and imagines that they have a better time. Secretly she fears that Paul will leave her for Renata, who, she believes, is more interesting, more attractive, more everything Paul could possibly want.

Helen is desperate for attachment but unaware of how difficult it is for her and how afraid of it she is. The emptiness she feels drives her to dream up an elaborate fantasy life. Before their first date, Paul was already the knight on the white charger who would arrive and make sense of her life. Always focusing her attention on others, as women are taught early in life to do, Helen was not able to feel her own strengths or to be secure in herself. In fact, she felt so unsure of her own needs and her own capabilities that she had created a world of imaginary relationships. She had no inner conception of her substance and strength. She had been brought up to live a life that could be jettisoned or suspended when the right man came along. She had been discouraged from carving out the shape of a life that would suit or reflect who *she* was; instead she had been taught to be dependent on the shape of her future man's life. Her dependent behavior became apparent in trivial situations. Now, on her own, she was obsessive about the kind of cutlery she should buy, unsure of what she really liked, and yet she pondered on how opinionated and sure of her design ideas she had been when she lived with Bob. Then, she had known just what she had wanted and hadn't been afraid to act on her ideas.

Because she felt unable to construct a real life for herself when she was on her own Helen came to live increasingly more in a fantasy world, one that she could have some control of. A paradoxical position had developed in which Helen, distanced from being able to define her real life, day-dreamed about a world that no one else could touch, where relationships worked out as planned, like in the movies, a world in which she had more control and felt safer and more secure.

This retreat into her inner world made her look at what was actually going on in her life with a rather skewed vision. She attributed the distance between her and Paul to another woman, Renata. But Paul had never been interested in a sexual relationship with Renata and was confused by Helen's jealousy. Helen had conjured up Renata as a threat to explain to herself the difficulties between herself and Paul. Much as she longed for closeness and intimacy she did not believe that she could trust Paul. Her desperate need for security and connection, coupled up with the fantasy world she was living in, meant that when she was faced with a real relationship that *did* offer security, *she did not know how to cope with it*. She is unable to trust Paul and sees (false) evidence of his desertion and his desire to get away from her at any point. She lives on tenterhooks, convinced that the emotional ax will fall and that she will be in the cold again.

Katie did not marry until she was thirty-seven, a year after meeting Pete on a trip to Europe. She had a very independent existence up to that time, working in a city agency. She had resisted lots of subtle and not so subtle pressure to marry sooner. She was determined not to settle, but to wait until she met a man who would stir up strong, passionate and loving feelings in her. For the first two years of their relationship they lived in a kind of honeymoon bliss. They returned from their jobs eager to see each other and with lots of energy left over to talk, walk, make love, visit with friends. They went away as often as they could afford to and were both taken up and delighted by their love. In the third year of being together, Katie, after long talks and planning with Pete, gave up her job and decided to risk going free-lance. She was very nervous about making the break from a safe and tenured job at a time of economic insecurity, especially as Pete earned quite a bit less than she at his job (they did not share money but they split the common expenses down the middle). But she was really fed up at work and wanted the challenge of starting up on her own. At the same time she decided to make the break, Pete, a union representative, was sent away on a week's course at short notice. Katie felt totally abandoned and wondered how she was going to make it through a whole week without him. She was frantically busy tidying up the loose ends at work. In fact, she only had one free night in the whole week. And yet she felt dejected, rejected, vulnerable, and scared at the thought of being on her own. Pete returned from the week all wrung out and tired. He acted withdrawn and distanced and it emerged later that he was actually feeling lousy about having left Katie for the week. Shortly after his return he got a cold, then he had an accident playing football. He was laid up at home for several weeks. Katie looked after him and was a tower of strength. He gradually got better but something significant in their relationship changed from that point on. For the next few years, Katie felt suspicious toward Pete and somewhat disdainful. She felt he couldn't really give to her as he had in the past and she wondered whether she was right about what had originally flowed between them. But the same time as she became somewhat contemptuous of him and even undermined his attempts to reach out to her, she became increasingly dependent on the relationship and felt more insecure than she had for ages. She kept looking to Pete for some sign that he still loved her and wanted her.

Katie discovered with an unpleasant jolt that she could maintain an independent stance as long as she wasn't in a close relationship. However, as soon as she had opened herself up in this relationship all her hidden and forbidden dependency desires came up and overwhelmed her. She was caught short by the intensity of her feelings of abandonment and rage at Pete. And she resented being so affected by these emotions. She'd been in women's groups and thought she was over feeling these kinds of disabling ways. The untimely separation, twinned with her leaving work, meant to her that she was out on her own without the cradle of support she felt would be there from Pete. Instead of being able to feel supported and be independent, she felt dropped, and became quite depressed. She felt utterly conflicted about her decision to go free-lance and felt awful when the volume of incoming work was lower than her target. She became very sensitive to feelings of rejection. Her confidence was shaken.

The unfortunate sequence of events had really destabilized Katie. She was overcome by feelings and anxieties that could not be explained by referring only to the actual circumstances. Nerves had been touched, feelings aroused, and a self-confidence shattered that went back years before Katie was involved with Pete. Under the layers of rationalities, consciousness, and life experience, Katie's unconscious asserted itself. With different players and different goals, Katie was reliving with Pete her very earliest childhood steps toward independence.

When we first come into the world we are utterly dependent. Without food, physical care or emotional sustenance we cannot grow. Emotional connection is such an important feature to our survival that babies in institutions without adequate personal attention cannot sustain their potential life force, they give up and die.[1] Whoever cares for us first and most consistently—usually mother—becomes our psychological umbilical cord. We depend on her for our very existence. We are merged with her and have no sense of where we begin or where she ends. What she gives us emotionally forms the very essence of our psychology and personhood. Her love and attention are essential foods that build our personality. They are as important as the physical nur-

[1] Rene A. Spitz, *The First Year of Life: A Psychoanalytic Study of Normal and Deviant Development of Object Relations* (New York: International Universities Press, 1965), pp. 278-84.

turing we receive to develop our bodies. She fills up our world, and our first experiences, pleasurable and painful, take place in an emotional context that she has created. We are enraptured by her, fascinated by and very much in need of her. Our personalities form a central core of their very uniqueness by what happens in those early interactions. How mother is with us, how she presents herself and the outside world, impacts on us in the most profound ways. Her enthusiasm for others will be communicated to us and we will be eager to make other relationships. A mother who is anxious will communicate that anxiety and we may face new relationships with unease and uncertainty.

Every mother has the almost impossible task of juggling her needs and the needs of her child. Every mother feels conflicted about her child's dependency on her, both enjoying and resenting it. Every mother worries about whether she is giving too much or too little. Every mother knows there are times when her child needs her desperately and times when she must let go. Every twentieth-century Western mother has absorbed enough popular psychology to feel responsible for the mental health of her child. Mother's care and attention build the foundation from which the child moves into the larger world. As the child is able to move around physically she or he explores the world around herself or himself, and lets mother know that she is needed in different ways. The physical growth goes hand in hand with changes in emotional development. The child gravitates toward other people, begins to look to them to fulfill some of the needs that mother provided before. The toddler is taking the first steps in the process of separating and becoming her or his own person. This is a process that occurs all through life but developmental psychologists have observed three or four distinct periods in which as children and adults we take a sort of emotional stock of where we are and try and move forward into some different emotional alignment. The first of these periods occurs between eighteen months and thirty months. It has been called separation-individuation.[2] The child who has embodied a reasonable degree of caring from her or his mother substitute begins to feel her or his own boundaries, own sense of self, own differences from this big person who is always emotionally present. The child begins to experiment with feeling this new sense of "me," of checking out its impact on the environment, of feeling her or his separateness from mother. The way the child approaches the larger world will depend so much on what she or he has absorbed up until this time. Some children are very enthusiastic, others tentative, others fearful, and others pursue new experiences in an almost wild fashion. Each new encounter is processed by the child. What happens "out there," when he or she is exercising separateness, affects how the next new encounter will be approached. With every endeavor at outreach, the emotional image of mother is present. . . . It is she that the child is distinguishing herself or himself from, and it is she who the child returns to for reassurance, to refuel, to touch home base.

When children make precocious attempts to separate from their mother, or later on in the adolescent phase of separation from their family grouping, we have to ask what is going on. What is propelling them out of the nest? Is it that they've had enough nurturance, plenty to feed on so that they are satisfied early, or is it that there is not enough of the right kind of nurturance and they need to seek it elsewhere, or is it perhaps that being merged itself was too sticky and cloying, not really satisfying?

In Katie's case, as we shall see with so many woman, her adult independence was a version of a survival tool she had developed when she was very little. Katie's mother was herself a rather needy person and went through a tremendously difficult time after Katie's birth in being responsive to her daughter. It was almost as

[2] Margaret S. Mahler, Fred Pine, and Anni Bergman, *The Psychological Birth of the Human Infant: Symbiosis and Individuation* (New York: Basic Books, 1975), pp. 3, 33, 34, 54.

though she felt jealous of the very attention her daughter demanded. She wanted someone to give to her, in an adult version, what she was giving to Katie. Katie's father, a busy doctor, seemed to have more time for his patients than for his wife or for his daughter. Katie's mother had become rather self-absorbed in her pregnancy, and her husband, feeling somewhat shut out, had retreated into building his practice and his reputation. Katie's mother felt exhausted. She longed to weep although she couldn't really say why. She felt tremendous urges to collapse but knew that her responsibilities toward her husband and Katie meant that she couldn't and she shouldn't. She tried to take herself in hand and suppress all her feelings of weakness and upset. She tried to be a good mother and attend to Katie's needs. But Katie's needs frightened her, *for they reminded her of her own forbidden needs.* Sometimes she was able to be responsive to Katie, to tune in absolutely to what she was wanting, and in giving to her provide a reassurance that all was well. At other times Katie's mother ignored her needs, just as she ignored her own. The situation would then escalate, with mother feeling increasingly more impatient and less able to give Katie what she needed. Katie might get distraught, her mother would not know what to do, and at her wit's end not be able to comfort her.

It was from this kind of insecure atmosphere that Katie, at age two, made her first attempts at separation. She showed her "independence" in many ways. She tied her own shoelaces, she fed herself, and as she got older she insisted that she walk to school on her own, that she prepare her own lunches and so on. These displays of "independence," in fact, hid her emotional dependency needs. At the same time she (unconsciously) discovered another way of hiding her own needs. She began to look after the needs of others, particularly her father's. Attending to others and denying her own needs were encouraged by everyone around her. One day when she was feeling miserable and let her mother see her unhappiness, her mother responded by suggesting Katie bake a cake for her dad. "Daddy will be so pleased." Katie was a good girl. She was never *self*ish. She was so giving and thoughtful of others. Katie, by this time, had embodied both the loving aspects of her mother's care and the confusing ones. A little girl who had impermissible needs now hid inside of her. She was going to approach the bigger world without the cumbersome neediness of her first years. She couldn't bear to feel her mother's rejection over again, as she did when her mother had ignored her or become frustrated with her and Katie had not understood what was going on, she had only felt its impact and had had to make sense of her mother's actions. Katie came to understand that she shouldn't rely on her mother too much, that she should "grow up" as fast as she could, or at least hide away her little-girlness. In quashing this part of herself, Katie grew up believing there was something vaguely wrong with what she wanted and with her needs.

When she began to look outside the mother-daughter orbit during the period of separation-individuation she was hoping either to have her needs met elsewhere or escape them altogether. Of course none of this was conscious, either on Katie's part or on her mother's. In Katie's inner world she resolved to bury the dependent wanting part of her forever. She thrust forward, taking up challenges with gusto, proving to herself that she could handle different situations. Every new situation built her confidence that she could cope, that she could take care of herself, that she didn't really need anyone. But every victory had its reverse psychic effect, for Katie became more and more distant from the little-girl part of her inside who had stopped growing, whose needs had been prematurely nipped in the bud, who still hungered for consistent attention. The little-girl part did not present itself directly, indeed she might never have become reacquainted with her if she had found enough challenges that could negate her existence. But when Katie fell in love with Pete, in her coming together with him, a part of her psyche unfroze. The woman with tight and rigid boundaries melted a bit and she let another person have a fundamental impact on her. In her closeness with Pete, her earlier feelings of closeness with her mother were re-evoked—both the positive and the difficult experiences. When Pete ''left her'' for the week at a point when she was moving out of her secure job at the city agency she felt as though she was being abandoned to face the world once again on her own. More than that even, she unconsciously felt as though his departure was some kind of punishment for her new work decision. Inside of Katie, his trip took on a different meaning. Katie felt that she was utterly unsupported, could not rely on Pete anymore, and that in some profound way, by his leaving at this point, the emotional cradle they had created together was irrevocably ripped. When he returned distant and then fell ill, Katie ''knew'' for sure she had been right. She was resentful that Pete was so wrapped up in himself that he was unaware that she was going through a difficult time. She felt she couldn't express her anxieties and fears about changing her job because his needs were so present. Katie felt she should never have let herself get that close to a man, they only disappoint you just when you need them. She found herself having to look after him at a time when she was feeling she would like that kind of reassurance herself. She felt he became terribly dependent just at the point she was needing his support to take on a new challenge. His illness put her into an old role of competently caring for another while having to suppress her own needs. When she came to one of our workshops on dependency issues to discuss the whole situation, she came in contact with how disappointed and upset she was about the course of events. She realized that she didn't want Pete to really do very much at all, she didn't really want to collapse, felt she could do *anything* if she only knew that he was really behind her. If he were then she could conquer any challenge. She realized that up until that fateful week and the ensuing illness, she had felt Pete was really there for her, concerned about her. She experienced his week's absence as a withdrawal and a rejection. It flung her back almost thirty-five years to feelings of utter loneliness and anxiety that she had suppressed. She felt that she had been dropped, that she had been pushed out rather than having gone forward from choice and with loving support. She was forced to deny her dependency needs once again. These needs were so forbidden.

Margaret is sixty-eight and widowed. She had described her forty-year marriage as miserable, her husband as ungiving, and her life as one experience after another of not getting what she wanted. For forty years she had led a fairly "independent" life, going out to work, attending meetings, traveling to see friends. She had long given up cooking for her husband or entertaining at home. She wasn't much of a grandmother to her only granddaughter. Although the first seven years of her marriage were tolerable, the following were not. For thirty-three years she shared a bedroom with a man who "grunted at her," showed little affection and even less interest in her life. For thirty-three years she dreaded the almost daily skirmishes, the anguish, and the lack of joy in her marital life.

Yet when Robert died, her world collapsed. She stopped eating, cooking, or shopping and spent her days gazing at the TV set. He left her comfortably off but she couldn't feel secure. Each day she clenched her bank book, called her accountant and counted her pennies. Her children, alarmed at the change in her, asked what was wrong. "Now that your father has gone, there is no point," she said with bitterness.

At twenty-four, after graduating from college and teaching for two years, Margaret had left her parents' home in New York to marry a talented Englishman, Robert, a professor of linguistics at London University. The idea of marriage to a foreigner had heightened the romantic flavor of the courtship for each of them. To a New York middle-class young woman, London and an Englishman spelled culture, excitement, history, and grace. Margaret saw her life unfolding with bigger horizons. Like many women of her background, Margaret had grown up at a time and in an atmosphere that directed young women to seek out their satisfactions and ambitions by marrying interesting men. An exciting life meant marrying a man who had an exciting life. Her pleasure was to come through sharing his joys and ambitions and by together overcoming his problems. Margaret approached her wedding with tremendous eagerness and joy.

If we look at Margaret's story with fresh eyes, new perspectives challenge the basis of our old perceptions, allowing us to see how the complex theme of dependency plays out in this relationship.

We discover a familiar story. Robert was the recipient, at least early in the marriage, of Margaret's care and attentiveness toward his career and general concerns. In fact, there were two people "working on," and committed to *his* having the fullest life possible. Margaret was not in a parallel position. Her own career ambitions were slowly dropped. Margaret wanted to be a lawyer but such a profession in England in the 1930s was closed to those who did not have the social connections made at private schools and the money to support a long apprenticeship. She received no support from Robert's family for her career attempts, as they were not much taken with the idea of a woman seeking a profession. Their opinion echoed that of many of her contemporaries, and Margaret found that she was somewhat at odds with Robert's friends, who felt a woman should look to the family as her central activity. Robert himself was concerned that Margaret find something interesting to do until they started a family. Margaret's teaching qualifications were not accepted in England and for the next several years she drifted into fairly boring work in interesting fields. She was a secretary to an antifascist organization, then to a cultural group that was putting on avant-garde musicals. She was frustrated, felt somewhat cheated, missed her friends terribly, and saw England turn gray before her eyes. Meanwhile, her relationship with Robert seemed to be deteriorating. They were squabbling quite a bit and she felt continually pushed aside. She longed to go back to America, to her family and friends and to law school, but Robert was reluctant to leave England. He felt guilty about her situation and didn't exactly know how to help her. But sadly he was unable to reveal to her how he felt, and instead he retreated away from her pain and upset. Margaret felt hurt, rejected, and abandoned. A part of her tried to accept the situation, a part of her made calculations—"I gave up so much to be here with him, and now he has the nerve to withdraw from me." A part of her turned bitter and resentful. She felt her life to be a disappointment. She loved Robert but she didn't feel he really understood her that well. She was worried that she was becoming a nag, someone who couldn't be satisfied.

Eventually Margaret had two children, a son and a daughter, born during the war. Robert was in the air force and for safety she took the children to the United States to her mother's home. She was very happy to be back in New York with family and friends. She felt they understood what she'd been going through in England, and they encouraged her to stay in New York.

But Margaret felt deeply tied to Robert. The physical distance between them brought out their strong love and concern for each other. They wrote to each other frequently and both looked forward to the end of the war and their reunion. As the time for Robert's discharge grew closer, Margaret fantasized about the happy family they would create and share. Her expectation of being together again, with the bumps behind them, excited her. She found herself longing to be with Robert and she got on the first passenger boat that would take her and her children back to England.

Within six months it was clear that the marriage was in trouble. Robert was an attentive father but not such an attentive husband. He devoted more and more of his spare time to causes and to his work. Margaret wondered what she was doing wrong. She craved more togetherness but was inevitably disappointed. Their sex life deteriorated and they fought regularly and with increasing bitterness. Every day Margaret resolved to not want so much from him. Every day she talked to herself about not being so dissatisfied, but every day she found herself hatching plans to go back home, seeing if she could muster the emotional strength to leave him. Every day she felt like a failure—she couldn't wholeheartedly stay and she couldn't leave. Her visiting girlfriends urged her to get a divorce but all she could say was, "What will become of me, I need him so!"

So why did Margaret stay in this disappointing marriage, lonely, cut off from her roots and her support systems, and increasingly miserable? We can begin to answer this dilemma by analyzing what really made her leave America in the first place. How was it that she came to be so attracted to a man who lived three thousand miles away that she would jettison contact with her friends, her family, and give up on having a career?

Margaret idealized her mother. To her Shirley was wonderful and uncriticizable. But to Robert and other observers, Shirley was a self-motivated and selfish woman. While she led a very active social life and was much loved by her friends, she had a rather distanced relationship to her husband and children. She rarely let their needs stand in her way. She expected the three children to look after one another and she played with them only occasionally, on a whim. Margaret learned an awful lot about coping with her own problems early on. Occasionally she would turn to her older sister for advice and comfort but essentially the two girls became women long before their time. The sisters were much admired for their independence and felt very proud that so much of the care of their little brother was entrusted to them. They were praised for being such good mommies. But why did Margaret carry around this strong image that her mother was so wonderful? Why did she call out for her in her sleep for years after her death?

The strong positive image that Margaret carried of her mother covered up a complex of painful, contradictory, unconscious feelings that Margaret had toward

Shirley. In fact, Margaret's childhood experiences were punctuated by hurt, disappointment, anger, and a sense of abandonment. Shirley was not that attentive, available, or nurturing. She was very involved with her work and committees, and was not very comfortable with her children and reacted to them rather inconsistently. They were very much her achievements, and were required to be attractive, polite, and responsive children. Behind this description of them was the psychological cost of their achieving this perfection. Margaret was a child who was discouraged from showing her needs. When she cried, her mother would say, "That's enough now." When she complained about being unhappy, mother implied that things couldn't be *that* bad. Margaret grew up hiding the part of her that was miserable, confused, tearful, and needy and developed a pleasing outside personality that mother was more prepared to relate to. Margaret's "outer personality" was capable and charming and other people responded warmly to her. The little-girl part was now quite at odds with Margaret's self-image and Margaret herself was unaware of how her early experiences shaped what she was hoping for and expecting in her adult relationships.

We can hold on fiercely to idealized images of our parents because when we were little we needed them so much. They, especially our mothers, were our first contact with the world, the bridge to other relationships. We looked to them to make sense of our experiences, to explain, comfort, make all right the hundreds of stimuli we encountered. A child is apt to think that it is her or his fault if needs go unmet or ignored by a parent, that there is something lacking about him or her or else the parent would be more attentive. It is a safer option for the child to preserve the parent as "perfect" and to see herself or himself as somehow naughty, silly, wrong, etc., than cope with the anxiety, anger, and upset that are aroused when a child feels insufficiently emotionally supported. It is frightening for a child to find fault with a parent. Even as we grow and need them less and expand our perceptions, our early images and the denial run deep. As a child, Margaret had often stretched out her hand to her mother for help and when mother was unresponsive Margaret took on herself the idea that she was perhaps asking too much. In this way mother's image as a solid, reliable figure remained intact, while Margaret battled inside of herself with the consequences of believing herself to be an overly needy little person.

What Margaret longed for from her husband, Robert, was a closeness and intimacy that she had never really experienced with her mother. In the early stages of their romance, when they were utterly fascinated and pleased by each other, their love for each other and their being loved took them out of themselves. This openness allowed them to feel very close, and in Margaret's case it opened up her desire for warmth and contact. She felt as though a great weight had eased when she met Robert, that she no longer had to hold herself so taut. She relaxed into the embracing hold of their relationship.

But as the relationship continued and Robert and Margaret were more assured of each other's presence, came to know each other better, and weren't so utterly riveted by each other, other aspects of their personalities came to the fore and things began to change. Margaret felt dissatisfied with Robert; he was less concerned with her and she had many reactions to his withdrawal. She felt angry and depressed about losing what she felt had been a precious contact between them. She held on to the memories of what had passed between them early on and longed to recapture the kind of love they had shared. But at the same time, dragging her down and more difficult to cope with, was the feeling of dread and disappointment that would come over her when she thought about how things would turn out. Like spasms of pain erupting, Margaret would come in contact with terribly upsetting feelings that things would always be this way, they wouldn't get much better, she couldn't or shouldn't expect them to, and that, for some reason, she was not going to have a happy marriage. When Margaret was in touch with these kinds of feelings she also "knew," in a profound way, that it would be no different for her with anyone else. She lived on a see-saw, balanced between two confusing experiences she couldn't bring together. She saw Robert as a potential prince, as a wonderful man who could be more responsive, caring, stimulating, and loving (if only she could get him to, or if only he would become so spontaneously), and yet she saw herself as a woman full of needs but doomed not to have them fulfilled. *She didn't believe that Robert or anyone would really love her.*

The logic of the individual psyche locked Margaret into a complicated and seemingly unsatisfying relationship. The disappointments in her earlier relationship with her mother, which had been so well disguised, were now reflected more openly in her relationship with Robert. Robert was idealized in ways similar to the idealization of her mother. There was an "if only" quality to what Margaret felt: "If only Robert would really listen; if only Robert would really understand." She held on to the notion that Robert would be her prince. Because she had never been allowed to be that dependent on her mother, she still yearned to be dependent, to be attended and cared for, but at the same time she didn't feel it was possible, she didn't think Robert would be able to give her what she wanted and needed. Inside of her she felt confirmed in the knowledge that she would be pushed away once again. So much of her life was spent in an emotional wasteland. Bitterness and resentment grew to fill the void left by her disappointment in love.

As we look with compassion at the stories of the other women on these pages and we follow the threads that connect each one's experience to another, we can't help but see that many women juggle with similar kinds of feelings of disappointment, anger, and loss. We are forced to the conclusion that there is something central to a girl's upbringing that affects how she approaches an intimate sexual relationship.

*   *   *

Sandra, forty, a French teacher, is married with three children. For the first ten years of her marriage she and her husband lived in the same house that her husband grew up in. She took on the responsibility of looking after her mother-in-law, who was somewhat infirm. For the last four years, she has been having a passionate and meaningful clandestine love affair with Daniel, a graduate student in philosophy. Sandra has been struggling with whether she should leave Leon, her lawyer husband, and set up house for the kids and Daniel. She feels she is living in a precarious situation and that her deceit and the unhappy relationship with her husband will have a bad effect on the children. She worries about whether she could support herself and about how it would hurt the children to lose daily contact with their father.

Sandra married a man who was still very attached to his mother. What she took as his maturity—he is twelve years older than she—was in reality an expression of his difficulty in separating himself from his mother. He married quite late, at thirty-eight, because he wasn't really able to make a commitment to another woman, but Sandra did not see this when they were courting. She fell in love with his worldliness and experience and felt that she would be able to learn so much from Leon and be stimulated by him. In reality Leon was not very available to Sandra. When his mother died, Sandra hoped that Leon would be able to move closer to her but sadly this did not happen. Leon seemed a bit more subdued after the death of his mother and Sandra was very protective of him, always shooing the children away from the living room so that they wouldn't disturb him. He could not talk much about the loss of his mother and what it meant to him. He remained rather remote and unreachable. Sandra was quite unhappy, for she hoped that after her mother-in-law's death they would be able to live as a much closer family, able to determine their own mealtimes and what they would like to do, appropriate to a youngish couple, now that they didn't need to defer to the wishes of his mother. After a year or two had passed like this Sandra took up with her lover. She was aching to come alive emotionally and was turned on by Daniel's energy and sexual interest in her. She felt appreciated and loved, but she did not believe the affair could possibly last, because she was so much older than Daniel and he would surely be "better off" with some-one nearer his age. She longed to be with him all the time but at the same time knew that there was something quite important to her in the present arrangement. She had an inkling that life would not necessarily become happier if she left Leon.

Sandra needed Leon, because she felt she needed a husband. Someone with whom she would have a daily relationship, someone who would know her as she was, now a middle-aged person, someone who would provide her with a sense of continuity and family. Sandra was dependent on Leon, but if we examine the content of the dependency we can see that Leon provided her with little more than a frame and a name for her existence. She was a working wife and mother. He provided her with a certain amount of economic security and legitimacy in the eyes of others. But he wasn't available for terribly much else. For love and contact she had to go secretly to another man who was able to provide those things. Sandra yearned for the close relationship she had with Daniel to transfer over to Leon, but her attachment to Leon was based in large measure on the fact of his un-availability. Sandra was involved with two men who were providing less than she wanted. Daniel had a his-tory of being involved with women who were involved with other men. When Sandra would discuss leaving Leon, Daniel would encourage her and then drop out of sight for a couple of weeks. Daniel had never been able to sustain a relationship with women who were single, and so Sandra knew that being with him rested on there being real safeguards and boundaries in their relation-ship. Sandra was attracted to men who could give only in limited contexts. She could never give all of herself to either of these men and feel really accepted. Sandra was restaging in her adult life an emotional play that she knew in her bones.

Her mother had been widowed when Sandra was three and was depressed for many, many years. She had not been able to be much of a mother to Sandra because she was so wrapped up in her own distress and later in a search for a new husband. When her mother remarried, Sandra was very happy. Her stepfather paid her lots of attention and was very interested in her development. Her mother, however, seemed to be jealous of their relationship, and Sandra came to feel guilty if he spent a lot of time with her, so as she grew up she avoided her stepfather in an attempt to avoid hurting her mother.

The emotional drama we grow up in can be, even without our knowing it, an imprint for life. It stays with us and shapes who we are and our expectations. What we observe in our parents' relationship to each other and to ourselves provides emotional signposts for what each of us feels entitled to get out of life. Unnurtured herself, Sandra saw her mother's unhappiness without a man and then observed her insecurity and jealousy with her new husband. Inside of Sandra this translated in the following ways. Sandra felt she had more good things in her life than her mother did, and she felt uneasy about this. At the same time she felt guilty that perhaps her mother had been deprived of meeting a man easily because of having a small child. The fact that Sandra's husband's mother lived with them was more than a passing coincidence. Caring for Leon's mother provided Sandra with the opportunity to make reparations to her own mother for the deprivation she perceived in her life. She very much had wanted her mother to be happy. The fact that Sandra was now involved with two men who were both unavailable was a replay of an emotional tableau she had known from her teenage years with her parents. Leon was a stand-in for her rather depressed and repressive mother, as was his mother; Daniel was the loving stepfather whom she was required to love secretly. Sandra could tolerate a situation in which she was always negotiating stumbling blocks because she had absorbed the idea that she would never have much more to look forward to. Love and close relationships were not especially safe harbors for Sandra, rather she knew that the love that accompanied intimate relationships was shot through with disappointment, pain, depression, longing, and guilt. There was a gap between what she so desperately wanted and what she felt she could have, and this gap was one she knew as well as she knew her own hand. It was so much a part of her emotional experience that she would have been lost without it. Sandra had grown up wanting something she could never name or put her finger on. She felt doomed to that wanting forever.

From the outside none of these women's lives would seem to be particularly troubled. But by shifting our focus ever so slightly we have seen that in important ways each of these women live lives of private anguish, of disappointment and quiet despair. Helen sought closeness but couldn't handle it; Katie hid her dependency needs; Margaret stayed with someone who gave her very little; and Sandra couldn't allow herself to be dependent on anyone. Each of these women has a substantial life separate from her relationship. And yet each woman feels she needs the relationship as the backdrop to her daily activities. Each of these women wants desperately to relate closely with a man. Each lives in a relationship that has come to humiliate that ideal. Mingled in with Margaret, Katie, Helen, and Sandra's pain and upset is a partial recognition, a sense that this is all they will get, should hope for or deserve. They fear they want too much. At the same time there is a rage, a rebellion, a fury, that in this most important aspect of a woman's life so little true contact seems possible.

We have to face a shocking and disturbing fact. The stories of Helen, Katie, Margaret, and Sandra are stories of ordinary, educated, working women. There is nothing exceptional in their situations. They are almost too familiar to take notice of. We begin to be startled, however, when we realize that their stories are duplicated by women in villages, cities, and towns throughout the United Kingdom and America and that millions of women live lives of appalling emotional sterility and dissatisfaction. In our practice time and time again we hear women speak of their inability to accept and live with their own needs. Many women even deny that they have needs. Other women who do recognize them feel shame about being needy. No woman expects to have her forbidden feelings accepted and responded to. Men and intimate relationships with men mean so very much to women because we have been brought up in a social sense to look to them to complete our lives. If we think back to Helen we can see that her experience with Paul is a common one. Many women feel themselves to be clinging and insecure in their intimate relationships. Even though there is no obvious reason for her to feel threatened, Helen imagines Paul has already disengaged from her, left her, and is really in love with another woman. For many women it is extremely difficult to believe that their partner actually wants to be with them out of his own choice and not because he is being held there. For these women it is equally as difficult to believe that a partner will be consistent in his love and that it will not diminish after the "honeymoon." Many women carry a feeling deep inside—a kind of preconceived knowledge—that inevitably they will be rejected and abandoned. In these pages we will hear the stories of many other women and see the varying ways in which women's feelings of dependency and intimacy are so problematic. We will also find out why this is so.

Helen's mother, like most mothers, raised Helen to become a caretaker of others and not to expect everlasting maternal nurturance for herself. Helen's mother did not have to transmit the same message to Helen's brother Arthur because of her unconscious knowledge and assumptions that he would have a woman to look after him throughout his lifetime. Arthur could expect continued "maternal" nurturance, and learning to provide it for others was not an essential task for his mother to teach him. The message to Helen, on the other hand, as with most daughters, was you must find a husband, a partner in life, but don't expect any man to be there for you like I (mother) am. Don't expect too much emotionally. Men are disappointments. Stand on your own two feet. Don't depend on anyone.

All women at some time have felt that "something" is missing if they weren't in a close relationship. As women, we may experience this feeling of lack in a general sense. Freud saw it in his women patients, and, with his patriarchal spectacles, symbolically named this phenomenon of twentieth-century women penis envy. As women psychotherapists listening to what women in therapy tell us, we hear this phenomenon in a different way and we understand it differently. We hear women talk about how they don't like to be on their own, that they long to be really close to another human being, and, yes, that there is something missing in their lives, a sense of a lack of completeness and wholeness. When we analyze these desires in terms of the individual history of each woman, and when we view her personal history in its social context, we see how dramatically the social world shapes our family relations, how children are raised and how parenting is conceived of and then how these weave together to create the particular gendered psychologies of women and men. We discover that a woman's inner feelings of inadequacy relate to the psychology of femininity, a psychology that has denied her adequate satisfaction of the very basic need to be dependent. Women, who on the face of it seem to be the dependent sex, are in reality involved in a cruel and unequal bargain that diminishes both men and women. Women are reared to provide for the dependency needs of others, to respond emotionally to their children, husbands, work mates, etc. Women develop emotional antennae that alert them to the needs of others. Women help those close to them process the disagreeable emotions that come up on a day-to-day basis. This process is so much a part of all our experiences that we may not even notice it. Women, almost instinctively, pick up on the concerns of others—including other women's—and find one way or another to help the person come to terms with whatever is at hand: *What is missing in women's lives is that they have never had the consistent experience of this being done for them.* In fact, a woman's very sensitivity to this issue comes not just from the role training she has received but is itself a psychological reaction to her own rawness. Her neediness, her desire to be understood, to be taken into account, alerts her to such need in others. A woman's emotional world is strewn with neediness, both her own, which she must so often repress, and that of others, which she anticipates and responds to. Rarely does a woman confidently report that her husband is able to anticipate and pick up the signals she emits about her emotional state and what she might be needing. Part of what each of us looks for in an intimate relationship is just this kind of interchange, and so women suffer terribly when they don't find their partners adept in such ways. But for this disappointment to be so profound and yet feel so inevitable to be almost anticipated at a subliminal level, it must resonate with emotional experiences, buried deeply and experienced in the past. For if women were just brought up short by the disappointments in their relationships with men and nothing more, they would either leave the specific relationships and look for another, more satisfying, one, or they would have, as many women are now choosing to do, abandoned the notion that many men are able to give at that level emotionally and look for loving intimate contact with women. But we know that many women cling tenaciously to unsatisfying relationships, hoping they will change, fearing that they won't, wanting to leave but feeling unable to. Partly this is out of desperation, as we have seen, but this desperation needs to be considered in the developmental picture of a woman's psychology we have sketched.

Women's experience that there is something lacking in themselves, and their deep desire for attachment, are part of the same phenomenon. There are two aspects to the lacking or missing feelings that so many women report. On the one hand is the denial of the little girl's dependency needs and on the other are the psychological consequences of this denial. The denial, or perhaps to describe it more accurately, an inconsistency in relating to a girl's dependency needs, produces in the girl feelings of lack of self-worth, of unentitlement and confusion. For if a need is denied, you come to feel all wrong about it and try to do away with it. When this happens early in life, the feeling that your needs are wrong translates into a feeling that you are wrong. The child feels that a part of her is wrong and unacceptable. In order to cope she tries to push aside her needy part and the part of her that knows what she wants. She attempts to pursue things that others will find acceptable. She buries her dependent part and in the process loses a part of herself. This part, now in hiding, suffers by not being related to, so that the little girl is both alienated from an important aspect of herself and further deprived of the nurturance she so desperately wants.

This alienation is then followed by a psychological dilemma. For if as an infant your dependency needs are not met properly, then it is difficult to go the next stage of emotional development—the process of becoming your own person. This developmental stage of separation and individuation will be approached either precociously as an attempt to flee the painful state of unsatisfied dependency need, with resistance on the part of the child, or at one of millions of shades in between. But whatever route the child takes in trying to negotiate her or his emotional growth, she or he will be hampered by being stuck, to one extent or another, in that early stage of needing. These needs may well be covered up, distorted, ignored, denied, or displayed in a cloying, clinging way. However they emerge, they are an expression of the fact that the person's dependency needs have *not* been met. Many people have misunderstood this phenomenon and rather have observed that a girl's attachment behavior and a woman's clinginess are a result of her dependent nature and how she is cosseted and encouraged in early childhood. But the girl, later the woman, is plagued by these needs precisely for the opposite reason. She suffers because her dependency needs were *not* sufficiently tended to when they needed tending. Unconsciously her longings, and the fact that she never "got enough," make it very hard for her to separate psychologically from her mother, because deep inside her, she still needs her very much. If she cannot have enough of her own mother, then she will bring those kinds of needs into other relationships. She will search for a mother in a friendship, in a marriage, always looking to find the missing piece that will let her get close, take in the nurturance she needs so that she can move on and become her own person. When women talk of there being "something missing," they are trying to explain mother's missing nurturance, which makes them feel less than whole.

We saw with Katie a common adaptation to the felt rejection of her infantile dependency. Katie developed a strong, independent personality that was ready to take on difficult challenges. In a sense, Katie ran away from her dependency needs until she tripped on them in her relationship with Pete. She turned their denial into a virtue, relying only on herself for her most important needs, and thus she did not risk rejection. But Katie's adaptation meant that for many years she paid the terribly high price of not being involved and close to someone, of not having a soul mate. Her passage through the period of separation-individuation was marked by a brutal psychological divorce from her mother and an attempted severing of herself from the caretaker she needed so much. In this sense, Katie did not so much become her own separate person organically but more as a result of the suppression of the little-girl part of her that had important needs that were not sufficiently responded to in infancy or thereafter. Because these needs were never adequately met their denial and repression gave Katie the feeling that something was missing inside her. When she opened up to Pete, that little-girl part emerged and she felt whole within herself. She was reacquainted with a part of her that had been buried and rejected for so long. In a sense she was getting back what she was missing, a core part of her personality. The difficulty came because unknowingly she invested the change in her working situation with attempting to redo a process that had been so painful to her thirty-eight years before. She was trying, now that she felt more whole, to go out on her own, with a sense of solidity, eagerness, and genuine confidence. She was struggling to be independent from a base of rich and loving support rather than in flight from a situation in which she wasn't getting her needs met. Her previous "independent" stance actually embodied a defense against her being in a state of acknowledged but unmet dependency. In leaving her job she had been trying to rewrite history.

Katie, Helen, and the other women we have met so far turned to men to meet needs that their mothers seemed unable to meet for them. What were these needs that their mothers didn't meet? What was the texture of the early relationship between these mothers and daughters? What do so many daughters feel was missing from their lives? Why do so many women feel disappointed? And what does it tell us about women's lives, women's expectations, and the effects of women being treated as second-class people?

In every case we have analyzed in our practice, in workshops, in one-to-one therapy settings, whether time-limited or open ended, with women of all ages who were raised mainly by their mothers, we have observed similar features in the mother-daughter relationship. Women who themselves are mothers come to therapy and tell of their experiences with *their* mothers. Women who are about to become mothers talk about the overwhelming presence of their mothers in their inner lives. Women who come to therapy to talk about their relationships with men, husbands, and fathers find themselves wending back to tell of the bittersweet emotions in their relationships with their mothers. Women we have seen are bursting to come to grips with this most powerful and fundamental relationship in their lives.

Without exception, all of these women share a terribly confusing experience. They feel tied to their mothers and "taken over" by them. They experience mother as interfering, expecting unreasonable things, and controlling. At the same time they feel pushed away (denied), not terribly well understood and not seen for who they are. They feel a tug-of-war between their needs and the needs of their mothers. We have heard this expressed so frequently that we have begun to call this the push-pull dynamic in the mother-daughter relationship. Mothers express enormous love and care for their daughters but this love is tinged with ambivalence that comes from their inner feelings about themselves, their femininity, and how they feel consciously and unconsciously about having a daughter. Mothers relate to their daughters in this fashion because they were related to by their mothers in this way. Inside each mother lives a repressed little girl who is still yearning for acceptance and love. Katie's mother's jealousy of what she was giving her daughter was only remarkable in that she was aware of these rather unpleasant feelings. Mothers are bound to have similar feelings for various reasons.

Because of the social position they occupy in our society, and because of the demands of the social role that goes with it, mothers, who are themselves second-class citizens, are in the unenviable situation of having to raise their daughters to step into the same shoes they occupy. In other words, it is the job of those who are themselves in a subordinate position to prepare the next generation of girls to take their place. This is cruel and ironic, for in mothering daughters women are in an almost impossible position. At the same time as they want and give emotionally they must prepare their daughters for a life in which the daughters will not be able to expect entirely equal rights. They need to help their daughters take up the feminine role and pitch their expectations at an appropriate level. Obviously this is not carried out in a particularly conscious way, or even in the bald sense we have just stated it. Mothering is a complex process that is much richer than any analysis of it could possibly convey. But mothering is also a social process, which is to say that it takes places under particular conditions, with certain demands and pressures that are shaped by larger forces that affect the very intimacy of the mother-child relationship.

One of the unwritten social practices that we are all complicit in, to one extent or another, is the unequal exchange of women's and men's dependency needs. The fact that women are raised to provide nurturance, care, and attention, to have others depend on them emotionally, and that boys are not, puts pressure on the mother-daughter relationship in four particular ways.

Firstly, mothers need to prepare their daughters to become givers. A woman's self-esteem suffers if she doesn't feel herself to be a "good giver." Consciously and unconsciously, then, mothers encourage and reinforce a daughter's moves to be caring, to develop her emotional radar, to be responsive. Mothers tell their daughters not to be selfish but generous, to pay attention to others' needs, to extend a hand (ultimately a lap), an invisible net of support.

Secondly, more than likely, mother is not receiving the kind of nurturance she wants in her marriage and so her daughter sees that mother and father's relationship is unequal. Mother may complain to her husband or she may comply. She may or may not convey her feelings directly to her daughter. Most daughters, however, pick up on mother's emotional dissatisfaction. They take in the idea that mother, whom she is like in gender and, therefore, like who she will become, wants things from dad that she doesn't get. Mother, a grown woman, is somewhat unsatisfied.

Thirdly, because mother is, to some extent, needy herself, she may look to her daughter for the emotional contact that is missing elsewhere in her life. In teaching her daughter how to give to others, she may, without even realizing it, offer herself as a candidate and their relationship may become burdened by needs that she doesn't have satisfied elsewhere.

Fourthly, mother herself is a daughter, and the daughter of a daughter. Her early development is marked by similar emotional shaping. Her mother had to teach her how to become a woman, and to hold back from wanting too much. These struggles resonate when she relates to her daughter. She feels the loss of her own mother's nurturance and may hope that her daughter will make up for it somehow.

For these reasons, mothering a daughter is fraught with particular strains. A mother may find it hard to respond without ambivalence. At times she can spontaneously love, give, listen, comfort, reassure, and encourage her daughter. At other times, she will withdraw, restrain, criticize and judge. The attitudes that accompany these actions may well be unconscious, a mother herself may be surprised at her inconsistent behavior toward her daughter. Many women speak of the shock they feel when they hear themselves sounding just like their own mothers when they are talking to their daughters. For example, Margaret would often hear herself scolding her own daughter, "Don't get upset," as though her mother were speaking her lines. A woman may feel herself to be a "loving" mother and be brought up short when she stumbles on the ways in which she curtails her daughter emotionally. These emotional factors entwine with the requirements of the role she is introducing her daughter to. The daughter becomes a potentially nurturing and dependable person for mother at the same time as she goes through a childhood with feelings of loss and incompleteness.

Because a woman may not have received enough nurturance in her life, which is to say that she may never have felt someone was really there for her, she may not feel a secure sense of self. She constantly will be looking for the person, the close relationship, that will give her security and fill up the emptiness. Sadly, men, to whom she turns, are not likely to have developed nurturing

skills. Looking at the way heterosexual couples fit together psychologically, from a woman's perspective, it
is as though women are, by upbringing, prepared for a
life in which they will lack the emotional contact they
desire so intensely. Restricted in the public world to one
degree or another, and disappointed in her close relationship, a woman will often have a child or children to
fill the void and to have someone with whom she is in a
dependent relationship. A child can be someone in her
life to whom she is undeniably attached. A woman can
give to her child and obtain a kind of satisfaction when
she projects herself into her child's shoes and then absorbs what she imagines the child is experiencing.

Readers may well feel suffocated by the concentration
on the mother-daughter relationship in these pages.
They may wonder where father is and how he influences
a girl's developing psychology and her adult relationships with men. For most of us father was not much
present in the crucial period of infantile dependency
when our personalities began to form. Few of us spent
more than a half hour or so with dad at the end of each
workday. For most of the week he was absent and it was
mother who gave to us and to whom we turned when we
wanted something. Father lives on the edge of the little
girl's world. He is always coming and going. His presence and absence affects the emotional atmosphere.
When he is around he receives mother's attention, when
he leaves that attention returns to us. Fathers relate in a
staccato fashion to their daughters, as do mothers.
Fathers can feel awkward handling little girls until they
are strong enough to rough and tumble. They may not
know how to comfort a baby's distress and without even
realizing it, pass a crying baby back to mother's arms.
From the little girl's point of view daddy is a mystery, a
powerful figure who is always leaving. She has no power
to keep him there or to get the attention she wants from
him. He is experienced as separate and different and
outside her immediate world. When, as a toddler, she is
separating from mother, father's position outside the
orbit attracts her. She may go to him to get what she still

needs so much, or she may approach him having hidden her needy part. But however she approaches him, his availability will be restricted by the demands of his social role. She will perceive that she cannot and should not expect too much of his time. She comes to feel somewhat powerless in her ability to make her father be there for her. Her relationship with him does not fill in the missing contact, for it too is marked by inconsistency. Father responds to her cuteness and charm, to her attempts to please him and engage him. He does not rescue her from the difficult aspects of her relationship with mother. He does not want to see her needy and wanting part. He does not offer her a real alternative. Her relationship with him is constricted in its own ways. It will affect all her future relationships with men.

Women live with painful feelings of deprivation; with longings for care, love, acceptance, and emotional contact. Each woman in her individual life and relationships searches to fill the emptiness inside and to make peace with this powerful theme of dependency and attachment.

In the following chapters we will explore the different ways women strive to satisfy their needs or to bury them. We will see the shapes men's dependency needs take and how the interplay of women's and men's dependency needs creates the essential dynamic of the couple.

■■
❖ ❖ ❖

The Great Taboo:
Men's Dependency

One hears very little said about the topic of men and
dependency. It seems that, by definition, men are not
supposed to be dependent. The very notion of masculinity excludes dependence. Men are seen to be the pro-
viders, the breadwinners, the protectors of women and
children, strong people with little emotional need upon
whom the family can lean. Women and children are
supposed to depend on men. Men are not supposed to
show their vulnerability, for it implies weakness—a
dreaded characteristic in a man. If a man shows vulnerability it shatters a myth. All of a sudden he is seen to
have fears and insecurities and to need reassurance and
comfort.

Women like both aspects of men's personalities.
Women like men's confidence in themselves and competence in the world. There is a sense of excitement in
the difference between a man's ''world,'' his way of
being, his maleness and a woman's own experiences.
Women help perpetuate the myth of the strong man, for
if there is a strong man a woman can imagine that she is
safe, that she is being cared for and looked after.

Women are also drawn to men's openness. Women talk about falling in love with a man and getting closer to him *because* he has exposed his vulnerable side. Showing himself, he "gives" a woman something. He has let her have a peek behind the mask of masculinity. She feels drawn to the person "inside." Maybe he's not so different, maybe he's not so scary, maybe he's not so big, maybe he can be playful, maybe he can be a friend, a mate.

A man may feel that he must woo a woman with his masculinity. When he first meets a woman he often feels under some pressure to perform with confidence and assertiveness. He "knows" that this is what women are supposed to be attracted to, and he wants to be successful in his love affairs. But at the same time, he is eager to have a woman with whom he can share another part of himself. It may be only with a woman that a man's emotional vulnerability emerges. It is taboo for men to expose that aspect of their personalities to one another, for it signifies emotionality and femininity. In friendships with other men a man may feel starved of intimate emotional contact. It is permitted for a man to be engaged emotionally with another man in an unequal relationship. That is, men can have emotional exchanges, as father/son, big brother/little brother.

Women *and* men suffer within a patriarchal culture. Developing into a person with appropriate gendered personalities means that from birth one is restricted in many areas of expression. For the little boy, growing up to become a man means being able to act in the world. There are clearly many benefits to learning to master the environment and to being related to as someone of substance, as a person with a certain degree of power. But there is a severe psychological price that boys pay for their ticket into patriarchy. A boy must disassociate himself from the world of his mother—his first world, the world of the home, the world of women. The boy must identify with his father, who, to some extent, is a stranger compared to the familiar feel and smell of his mother. The boy must be like his father and go into the world. But here a psychological problem presents itself, for in the first year of life the infant boy has merged with his mother, has taken aspects of her personality into himself in the developing of his own personality. Mother is inside of him; she is a part of him. Then he goes through the psychological developmental phase of separation-individuation and begins to experience his separateness from mother and his own boundaries. Simultaneously he is confronting gender awareness, which, for the little boy, may be an equally difficult psychological task. At the same time he is dealing with the understanding that he is different from mother, he begins to identify consciously with father because of their shared gender. Mother and father are different. He is like his father. He is not like his mother. At the point at which (and this is as early as age two) he begins to identify himself as a boy, like his father and different from his mother, he must keep her femininity out. He must begin to develop a sense of himself as different from her. As the boy grows, this dynamic solidifies. He is a boy; he plays with boy's toys; he won't play with dolls and dishes; he won't wear aprons; he plays with tools and guns; he plays "going out to work" instead of house; he wants to be like daddy. Being like daddy translates into a denial of the ways in which he is like mother and a denial of the fact that she is already a part of him. He must act in male ways—he must not cry; he must try to win, to come in first, to succeed. His sense of himself comes to depend on his achievements, his mastery. His developing personality is male. His self-confidence rests on his competence with the games he plays, life at school, etc. He is encouraged to compete. He is encouraged to win at all costs. He feels terrible if he loses at a game; it upsets something inside, it shakes his confidence.

Mother is there encouraging him on. She is a part of his experience as he relies on her support and love. Mother, caught in the web of patriarchal parenting, cooperates in the creation of a split in her son's personality. Unconsciously her son's gender affects the way she relates to him. Mother relates to her son with all of her own unconscious beliefs and assumptions about who boys and men are and can be in the world. At the same time as she feels proud to have produced a son, a little prince, she is resentful of the life opportunities he will have because he is a boy and that were denied her. She encourages her son to be a man. In so doing mother unwittingly colludes in her son's psychological negation of her. Who he is rests on his denial of what he has taken in from her, of how much he is "like" her. Men's psychology contains a split—the part that is seen in the world, acts in appropriate male ways; and the part that is buried deep in the unconscious in the earliest infantile memories of emotional, physical, psychological merger with mother.

In intimate relationships with women this hidden part of the man's personality gets touched. In connecting closely once again with another woman a man may let down some of the defenses he has had to construct. But these particular defenses are a central feature of a man's psychology—he unconsciously feels he needs them in order to carry on in the world, in order to continue to know himself. These defenses developed early in life and are a part of his psychic structure. Letting down these defenses, for many men, seems an impossibility.

Paradoxically, however, although men must deny aspects of mother that are inside, they can continue to rely on mother's support and care. A boy can feel secure in having his mother look after him, clothe him, prepare his meals, clean up after him, encourage him, nurture him. More importantly, he can look forward to this in later life from another woman, his wife, who will replace his mother. As we have illustrated in chapter I—this experience is not parallel for the girl.

We now begin to get a glimmer of the true picture of men and dependency. For although men's dependency needs are hidden in the culture at large, in fact, men's dependency needs are more continually met. Both internally, psychologically, as well as externally in the world, there is a camouflaging process taking place. The internal camouflage is the denial of mother inside—a denial of men's original dependency on a woman to survive. This internal camouflage is aided by psychological defenses that aim to maintain the masculine sense of self.

The external camouflage is the ideology that states that women are dependent, weak, and helpless while men are independent, strong, and autonomous. Here there is a camouflaging of men's continued dependency on women emotionally, sexually and physically.[1]

Men depend on women in both material and emotional ways. How often do we hear women say that they hope they die first because their husbands wouldn't be able to survive without them? That a man won't be able to boil an egg or know where anything in the house is without first asking his wife. The women's liberation movement has opened the door of the household, looked in and exposed the whole issue of domestic labor. But so far feminists have looked at one aspect of that labor—the unjust power relations that have women doing all of the unpaid domestic labor, which is then undervalued. We've seen male privilege as husband sits back with his slippers on watching the television while wife endlessly cleans and cooks. What we have not yet analyzed about that situation is the way in which men continue to be dependent, like boys with mothers who look after them and cater to their physical needs. Especially today, when more and more women are either forced to or choose to work outside the home, the inequity cries out. Men continue to have a "mother"; women do not. From boyhood to manhood, although men may be enormously productive outside the home, in the domestic sphere their lives remain constant. Boys have their food bought and cooked; their clothes laundered and ironed; their homes attended to, cleaned;

---

[1]This is one of the critical mistakes Colette Dowling makes in her book *The Cinderella Complex*. Ms. Dowling never looks at the way men's dependency needs are catered to and more regularly satisfied than are women's, thereby enabling men to go out into the world and be "independent" and successful. They do that with the security of a home base.

their mothers' shoulders to cry on; and their mother's encouragement about who they can be in the world. As men with wives in an unchallenged patriarchal household they have their food bought and cooked; their clothes laundered and ironed; their homes attended to, cleaned; their wives' shoulders to cry on; their wives' encouragement about their success in the world. There is a continuity in boys' early dependency experience that extends on into adolescence and manhood. These examples of dependency are examples of material and physical survival. But they have their emotional complement. Mother is always there. The person who was raised to become a mother, a nurturer, and emotional caretaker of others is there for him. Boys can live with the expectation of continued maternal nurturance, first from mother and later from a wife. At the same time as men acquire power in the outside world—by being born male in a patriarchal culture—they continue to be looked after (as children are) at home.

As we have seen, developmental psychologists have observed that in order to achieve successful autonomy, separation, and a secure sense of self, the toddler must have a secure home base. That is, the child must feel that as he or she steps out into the world and away from mother that mother will not disappear; that she will be there as the anchor, the safety net of love and encouragement. With this security the child can expand her or his world and come to feel the world as a safe place and that it is okay within that world.

In looking at little boys', and later men's, experiences we find some resonance with "healthy" developmental theory. For although boys have the difficult task of separating from mother psychologically, identifying with father, and developing a sense of themselves that is different from mother, they do not lose mother. They do not have to give her up or, more importantly, they do not have to give up the expectation of and indeed the maternal nurturance itself. They have the *psychological* task of separation (as do girls, but for whom it is more difficult to separate from the same-gendered person) but they do not have to let go emotionally of their need for a woman to continue to care for and look after them.

In the same way that women's labor has been invisible in society, so too has men's dependency been invisible. Women say of themselves, "I don't do anything. I'm a housewife." And men say of their wives, "She's got nothing but free time, she stays at home all day. She doesn't work." In the same way that men have had to deny "mother" inside of themselves psychologically, so too is men's dependency on women denied. Revealing men's dependency needs threatens a deeply held inner conception of the way things are for both men and women. Recognizing a man's need for a woman brings up for all of us the power of women. In our society, where by and large women raise children, women are very powerful people. In our memory we hold an image of a big person who held, fed, and protected us. So although women's nurturing and "mothering" abilities are thoroughly undervalued, we see that for men and women alike a woman was an extremely powerful person in their lives. If we accept that men are in fact dependent on women emotionally we need to go a step further and look more closely at men's attachment to women.

Frank is a legal aid lawyer. He is thirty-four years old and has never been married. He has been involved in various relationships with women since the age of seventeen. The relationships have lasted from several dates to two- and three-year relationships. There was a pattern in how the important, long-term relationships ended. Several of the women Frank dated he stopped seeing because he wasn't interested enough. In his three-year relationship with Joan things started out great, they both were in love and excited about being together and then, gradually, difficulties began. They began to have regular fights—some of which were resolved well, but others left a residue of bad feelings, which took away from the initial joyful feelings of love. Frank began to feel that Joan didn't understand that he had been under a lot of pressure at law school and that he had to devote time and attention to his work. Joan complained that he didn't think of her, that he didn't "court" her anymore, and that he treated her like a piece of furniture. He felt furious with her for her complaints and "nagging," and began to feel that she was only an additional pressure in his life; making him feel bad, angry, and taking up too much of his energy, which he needed for his career. They decided to end it.

After several years of dating, Frank met Mindy. He was very attracted to her both physically and intellectually. Mindy was a social worker committed to the same things he was committed to—things that led him to work for legal aid. Frank felt more mature, felt that he had settled into his profession, that his experiences with women had been good for him at the time. Frank was optimistic about developing a committed relationship with Mindy. He knew that he wanted a family and it seemed that maybe he should start to think about this more seriously. For the first year the relationship progressed almost effortlessly. Frank was in love, excited, and filled with happiness that he had found a woman he could really love. Frank thought about Mindy throughout each day and eagerly awaited the evenings when they would be together. He took Mindy to his favorite restaurants, bought good bottles of wine for their evenings in. They decided to live together. Frank was happy and felt that Mindy, too, was happy. He felt confident that she loved him. Frank felt he now had everything he dreamed of—his law work and a woman he loved who loved him.

Two years later Frank and Mindy came to us for couple counseling because they were on the verge of splitting up. Why? Mindy felt that Frank was always absorbed in his work and that he no longer understood her or knew what was going on in her life. She felt he no longer gave to her or loved her. Frank did not understand this at all. He knew that he still loved and wanted

Mindy and although he agreed that they had become more distant, he did not feel there was a loss of love. It wasn't until Mindy told him that she was thinking of leaving that he became fully aware of how serious the situation was. At first he blamed Mindy and thought that it was because she was not satisfied by *her* work and was looking to their relationship for too much in her life. He thought this was "neurotic" on her part. But deep inside Frank was frightened because this seemed to be a repeat of his relationship with Joan. He was scared that there was something wrong in the way he was in a relationship. Mindy seemed to say many of the things Joan had said: how she felt ignored by Frank; that the time spent at home more frequently was spent with Frank looking over his work, preparing briefs, etc., and that when Frank wanted to relax he put on the television, watched sports, read the newspaper. In couple counseling Frank said he felt Mindy's complaints were so elusive, he really didn't know what she wanted from him.

Frank and Mindy's experience has been echoed by many couples. Women complain of men taking them for granted, of men not "knowing" them deeply or not understanding them sufficiently. Men, meanwhile, often feel bewildered by this and don't really understand what it is women are talking about. They think women are just complaining, "bitching," "nagging." "What *do* women want?"

If we unravel the psychodynamics of Frank's attachment to Mindy we see one example of how men's psychology and their dependency come into play in relationships with women. At the beginning of the relationship Frank wanted Mindy; he was attracted to her personality, looks, and intellect, and had the desire to be closer to her. In the courting behavior Frank gave a lot of himself. He was extremely interested in listening to Mindy, in hearing about her work, her personal history, the way she saw the world, etc. He was building an emotional attachment to her and hoping that she would reciprocate the feelings. He wanted Mindy to desire him as much as he desired her. As their relationship developed Frank continued to appreciate Mindy. He was happy to be going home to her, looking forward to sharing stories of the day each had had. Frank felt that Mindy understood him and cared tenderly for him. He allowed himself to be vulnerable with her; to tell her of his fears and worries about his work, about himself. He felt accepted by Mindy, and her love provided him good feelings about himself, which he took with him out the door each morning. He needed and loved Mindy. He felt close to her and open. What was the problem? Because their relationship had such a strong foundation and because Frank felt so secure in his home life, he was, in fact, taking Mindy for granted. He was unaware of his dependency needs because he was satisfied. Frank unconsciously felt that he could depend on Mindy being there with him always. His attachment to her resonated at a psychological level with what he had always been raised to expect: a woman to love him and be with him. He was content and in love. That is why Mindy's statement of feeling he didn't love her seemed ludicrous to him. Of course he loved her.

As we have seen in chapter I, girls, because they must give up maternal nurturance, have in their psychology the anticipated loss of a nurturing person. Just as a young boy feels mother is there, regardless of how much he gives back to her, so Frank came to assume that Mindy would be there no matter what. In couple counseling Frank realized that on an emotional level he did stop "courting" Mindy, that he didn't listen to and give her the emotional attentiveness and care he had at the beginning of their relationship. He realized that it had to be a conscious process for him to relate intimately because left to his own unconscious motivations he would not struggle to relate emotionally. He saw where he had to push himself to overcome his own socialization to a male emotional role. He had to learn how to give and how to be emotionally nurturing to another person.

*   *   *

Rubin is thirty-six years old. He feels that his relationships with women are repeated disasters. For some reason, unbeknown to him, Rubin falls in love with women who are unavailable. He doesn't know why he does it, but inevitably he becomes attracted to women who are married or involved with someone else. Rubin's friends have introduced him to single women but none have ever really engaged him. It's as if the spark is missing. Rubin experiences time and time again situations at work, at parties, and at social gatherings where he becomes attracted to a woman who is with another man. Rubin is a lab technician and several times he met women whom he liked working at the lab. There was Anne, who worked on the fourth floor. Rubin noticed her and finally invited her to lunch. She accepted and Rubin found himself unable to think about anything but Anne for days before the lunch date. It was a big disappointment when Anne told him that she lived with Jack. Then there was Alison. For months Rubin was aware of Alison in the radiology lab. Every time something had to be delivered from his department to her lab, he leaped at the chance to make the delivery so that he could see Alison. She seemed very friendly to him. Rubin fantasized about her before drifting off to sleep. He imagined he and Alison together and in love. Finally, after several months, Rubin overcame his anxiety and asked Alison if she'd like to go out with him. She accepted. It turned out that Alison had recently broken up with someone. She was still upset about the ending of that relationship. Rubin felt sympathetic and listened to Alison and talked with her about her old boyfriend. After a month of dating, Alison told Rubin that she was going back to her former lover. She was very sorry but couldn't help it; she still loved him. Rubin was distraught. He felt he would never have a woman he wanted. He felt he had failed again.

Rubin's experience illustrates another dynamic in men's dependency problems. Rubin constantly finds himself in a familiar drama. The cast of characters is a woman, a man who the woman is somewhat attached to, and Rubin. Rubin is always psychologically on the line; that is to say there is a goal that is extremely difficult to achieve because there are significant blocks in the way, and Rubin's sense of adequacy and sense of self is connected to whether or not he can reach his goal. What is this drama that Rubin and so many men play out over and over? Let's first look at it historically and analytically.

As an infant the boy "has" mother. They are the couple. As the boy gets a bit older he comes to see that, in fact, mother is also attached to another man. This is psychologically jolting for the little boy, who has to learn to negotiate this new triangle. He has complicated feelings about father. He sees the powerful position father maintains vis-à-vis mother. The boy is encouraged to identify with his father, to form a bond, an alliance based on their shared gender. He looks forward to being like father and hopes one day to have "a girl just like the girl that married dear old dad."

In Rubin's case his mother was a distant person. She found it difficult to openly show love to her children; she was withdrawn emotionally. This affected Rubin and his sister differently. For Rubin was able to "escape" his early merger with his mother by turning toward his father, who was more emotionally accessible, and identifying with him. Secondly, Rubin would move away from the pain of his early feelings of deprivation by looking ahead to a future in which he could have a woman love him "better."[2] It is as if Rubin unconsciously lives with a piece of unfinished business all the time. He needs to feel loved, he needs to be shown that he is worthy. He tells himself that the reason he doesn't have this is because there is another man who is getting the love. He struggles painfully time and again to win the love of a woman. The test is out of

[2] This was not the same for Rubin's sister, whose identity was caught in the merger with mother and who could not have the expectation of a "better" mothering experience in the future.

proportion of "normal" loving—available women, women who like him immediately, won't do. They can't repair the damage inside. They can't fit the role that will eventually rewrite the drama with a good ending. If a woman is available and interested in Rubin there is no fire, no sparks, no challenge. Unconsciously he tries to be the winner in the triangle so that he can undo those painful experiences of rejection. But alas, he finds the rejection repeated again and again, only to confirm what he feels and fears inside: that he will not be loved and desired by a woman, that he will feel painfully alone and outside. His dependency needs were not satisfied early on in life and he is hungry and feels unworthy.

For other men, the unavailable woman may signify something else. There are many men who feel frightened of an intimate connection to a woman, who feel that their dependency is potentially too great, or who feel that they must maintain their separateness because in actuality their psychological separateness is shaky. The unavailability of a woman provides protection. Such men can "go after" a woman, fantasize about her, feel sexual feelings in relation to her, feel love for her—at a distance. There are different reasons why a man may feel he needs a barrier between himself and a woman. He may feel that women are controlling, and involvement with a woman means giving up an inner sense of freedom. He is attracted to women and pursues them with great enthusiasm, but intimacy and commitment make him feel trapped. He must maintain his independence in order to maintain his sense of self. Men such as these may have had mothers who held on to them, clung to them, needed them too much. They had to break free of their mothers and that was a difficult struggle (maybe they haven't yet succeeded), and so involvement with a woman seems dangerous. Popular culture feeds that particular image with expressions such as "she hooked him," "she caught him," and the like. We hold images of free animals being roped into domesticity.

Many men manage to negotiate this fear by half measures. Some can be in a committed relationship and enjoy the intimacy and security such a relationship can provide, but must at the same time have affairs outside of their marriage. Others won't have affairs but find themselves looking at and attracted to other women in a rather obsessional way, in order to maintain a sense of autonomy—of life outside of the couple—of freedom. There is also something exciting about the newness of another woman, a sense of not yet "possessing" this "object"; of knowing one's wife very well and of feeling secure in "having" her and so the excitement of "getting" her is gone. This sense of going after something, conquering it, mastering it, possessing it, establishing control is all part and parcel of a boy's socialization to the male role. Whereas women often seek a sense of themselves within the couple and from attachment to their partner, men may need to maintain and secure a sense of themselves from outside.

The phenomenon of "don't disturb daddy" is familiar to many of us. Men's boundaries are sensed and respected by others. A man can create a separate enclave even within his own home. We see this most easily with dad reading the newspaper or watching news and sports on television; dad "working" on something either brought home from outside or a household repair of some sort; dad taking a nap and everyone being instructed by mother to tiptoe around and not disturb him. There is an acceptance that men need some privacy and that entering those invisible boundaries is serious business with serious consequences for the intruder. This rarely is the same with women. (Recently women are raising this as an issue—to be taken seriously when they are working, that they are busy and not to be disturbed.) Children tend to go to mother for all sorts of things and don't give a second thought to "disturbing" her when she's cooking, cleaning, reading, watching TV, etc. Men determine and are more in control of their availability.

* * *

Alan and Marjorie are both writers and work at home. Alan has had two novels published. Marjorie has had less public recognition for her writing although she has published several magazine articles and short stories. They are both in their early thirties and do not have children. They have separate rooms in which they work. Alan begins by 9:00 A.M. and absorbs himself quite thoroughly in his writing. He comes out of the room for an occasional cup of coffee, a sandwich, a short break. Sometimes he looks in on Marjorie at her work, says hello, chats for a few minutes. Marjorie finds herself responding and taking short breaks when Alan does. Her concentration is easily broken. It's as if she's always ready to relate if she is made aware of Alan's presence. She cannot keep him out of her awareness. On the other hand, Marjorie looks in on Alan whenever she takes a walk from her desk. If she sees that he is absorbed working usually one of two things happens. Marjorie may not say anything to him for fear of disturbing and angering him or if she asks if he wants a cup of coffee his response often is to acknowledge a yes or no and remain concentrated in his work. Even if Marjorie brings the coffee to him, he nods or says thanks and carries on. The presence of another person does not have the same effect on Alan as it does on Marjorie. When he is within his own world and boundaries, he can stay there; the coming and going of Marjorie does not disturb his equilibrium.

Alan's ability to maintain his boundaries is one of the beneficial differences in being raised with a male psychology. Yet, the consequences of being raised a boy are equally severe as those of being raised female. First of all we suggest that a man's separateness, and therefore his ability to feel like a person in his own right, rests on a bizarre reversal of identification and power. He realizes that he is not like mother (up until that time the most powerful figure in his life) and in seeing himself as different from her, he must deny the power she has. Social realities of men's power mean that the boy sees his father's power at the same time he is coming to identify with him. There is an intricate process whereby the social laws of patriarchy, the position of the mother, and the developmental stage of psychological separation and gender identification weave together, and unbeknownst to him the boy is caught in the web of patriarchal power relations and must find his place. We suggest that in his unconscious there remains a memory of mother's power and also a memory of his denial of that power and of his own internal conversion of those power relations. Therefore, buried in the unconscious is also a fear as well as admiration for women.

Men's ability to be "separate," then, rests on a firm set of defenses constructed to maintain a sense of himself as male. These strong defenses and boundaries also represent a fragility in his psychology—it is unintegrated. In other words, there is both a "healthy" sense of autonomy, of "keeping people out," and a "neurotic" defensive distancing, of keeping people out so that they don't come too close, don't get inside, don't discover. . . .

Men may appear to be narcissistically overinvolved and this may reflect the split in their personality in which they are caught up and trapped inside of themselves and therefore have a dynamic relationship to themselves. Growing up a boy and developing into a man in patriarchal society cause splits in men's psychology that can be crippling to mature emotional exchange in adult relationships. Men often feel uncomfortable in situations in which there is open emotional intercourse. They may feel embarrassed, nervous, awkward at the outward display of emotionality or uncomfortable about what is expected of them. They may retreat into their other world, the world of work. In times of emotional crisis the job of comforting, sympathizing, or dealing with the upset is most often turned over to women to handle. Even when it is a member of a man's family who is in the distressing situation it is the wife who deals with the event. Men look to women to provide the social grease. What is remarkable is the way in which men's dependency on women is both invisible and blatantly apparent. We speak of the hostess who enables everyone to feel at ease, or the wife who calls her mother-in-law, sisters-in-law, etc., and maintains the family nexus. We say, "What would he do without her?" but we fail to see this as an aspect of men's dependency on women.

Being raised as a boy in our society hampers men in their emotional relationships. Responding to another's emotional needs, giving of oneself in nurturing ways, is a potential that all human beings possess. But this potential, like so many others, must be developed. It is not formed at birth, it is not natural and inevitable because of one's biology as male or female. In our culture nurturing becomes woven with gender and femininity. "Mothering" is something girls are continually given the opportunity to develop in themselves. Girls are given dolls to practice on, girls are given tea sets in order to rehearse feeding and serving others, girls are continually told to "be nice," which for a girl means not fighting, letting others have their way, being selfless. We know that this training in a rigid sex-role society is extremely oppressive to girls, but nonetheless girls are developing as part of themselves a human potential of nurturing and giving and thinking about others. Boys are discouraged from developing that part of themselves. In the same way that the outward, active, achieving, daring, and energetic aspects of girls' personalities are hampered and restrained, so too are boys' emotional, caring, gentle, nurturing, relational aspects of their personalities denied growth and development. Boys who show interest in playing with dolls, or even playing with girls for that matter, are considered "sissies"—a curse of being like a girl—so deep are the taboos against boys' continued identification with mother and femininity. Boys receive direct prohibitions about developing nurturant characteristics. Perhaps more significant in terms of men's psychology is that aspect of mother that boys embody that is not fostered and developed, but repressed in the unconscious, where it takes on a much deeper and scarier meaning.

"When my wife had our first child I felt very afraid to hold the baby. It wasn't that I was afraid I'd drop her or anything, it was more that I felt nervous, ashamed. I noticed that when I was alone in the baby's room I felt relaxed in holding her. In fact, I loved it. But as soon as someone else came into the room or if we were in a situation where there were other people I just felt too uncomfortable. I would want my wife to hold her. One afternoon we had my brother and his wife and their kids over and another couple who are friends of ours. We all were sitting in the living room and my wife was making something in the kitchen. Jessie [the baby] was crawling on the floor and started to cry. I went to pick her up to comfort her and I saw my brother watching me. Suddenly I felt overwhelming anxiety. I managed not to show it but later that night I told my wife about it. As we talked I suddenly had the memory of playing house with my next-door neighbor. I was about six years old. There were two girls living next door and the three of us were playing with dolls, dressing them, giving them bottles and things like that. We heard someone laughing outside and when I looked up there was my brother, who was three years older than me, and a bunch of his friends laughing and pointing and calling me sissy and saying, 'Ralph plays with dolls, Ralph plays with dolls,' over and over. I wanted to run away and hide forever."

Boyhood is filled with repeated messages that being a boy means *not* being like a girl. Boys' friendships develop within an atmosphere of boys *doing* things together: moving, being active, thinking about how things work, watching men compete in sports, etc. Friendships with other boys are crucially important and having a good friend, someone to play with, rely on, is very much needed. But by adolescence we already see where male friends have difficulty in giving one another what they need. Feelings of insecurity, anxiety, fear, which get aroused during adolescence when the young man is experiencing his sexuality and his new interest in girls, are rampant and yet talking about feelings (especially those with "negative" connotations, implying weakness) is something boys are ill-prepared to do. In adolescence we see the split in men's psychology take on a stronger defense as the young man has to act in a certain way in the world in order to be accepted by his peers—that is, he must act confident, cool, experienced in love, when he may be feeling utterly terrorized inside. At this point in his development, when he is struggling to make the transition from boyhood to manhood, exposure of inner feelings is extremely dangerous—after all, he is trying to show that now he really is a man.

Girls have a different experience. Because girls are allowed to have emotions and upsets and insecurities, adolescence is a time when they too need their friends. Girls spend much of their adolescence talking to one another about their pains and woes of love affairs, fights with parents, changing bodies. Girls use their relational skills to be with one another.

Because of this imbalance, girls continue to develop their nurturing potential while boys are locked inside of themselves. Something important is learned about emotions through this experience. Because girls are surrounded by emotional chatter, dramas, sagas, they come to see that emotional upsets pass. That is, upsets are there, quite intensely, are talked about, lived through with a friend, and then over. Learning to sit with someone else in their upset, listening and trying to understand what it is they are going through (getting into their shoes, so to speak), is another critical lesson in nurturance. Adolescent boys miss yet another chance to develop skills of equal emotional exchange, of giving and taking. The gap gets wider and men come to be frightened of emotions.

The imbalance in the learning of nurturant behaviors means that men come to feel bewildered and confused about what they're supposed to do when demands are made of them to respond to their lovers' emotional needs. Like Frank the lawyer, many men hear complaints by their partners that they are not giving in the right ways or that they don't listen adequately. Men feel these criticisms and more often than not respond with anger and frustration. "What *do* women want?" "I don't know what she wants from me. She's driving me crazy." "No matter what I do it's never the right thing. When Alice is upset she tells me I make her feel worse. I try to make suggestions about how she can get out of feeling depressed and she says I'm all wrong and that I don't understand anything. It's infuriating." These kinds of statements are familiar to many heterosexual couples. A woman can't understand or believe that a man doesn't know what she wants; she feels he's just withholding and being impossible. The man, on the other hand, feels the woman is being impossible, insatiable, and undermining. Nothing he can do is right. What happens at that moment? (In chapter III we will look closely at the couple dynamic.)

Men expect to be listened to. It is in the very fabric of their experience that they can look to a woman to listen to them. Mother listened when they were boys, girlfriends listened when they were adolescents, and women listen now that they are men. Men look to women to validate themselves. They see themselves reflected in the eyes of the woman who looks adoringly. Women are in awe of men's powers and status (consciously as well as unconsciously) and their awe is transmitted in the gaze of the adolescent girl and later the woman.[3] Men need that attention and confirmation. Very often men don't even want women to respond or give advice about something they are talking about—they just want to be listened to in the way their fathers were listened to. To be a man is to command attention and authority.

Precisely because men have the continuity in experience of being listened to their experience of the way things are is just that; that is to say, the dynamics of being heard but *not* of listening back in the same way creates its own reality. It's not that there's something wrong or missing, because there isn't something missing

---

[3] A woman gets this kind of attention and appreciation of herself only through being able to present herself as attractive and appealing.

for men. It's quite tragic that often it is only through the loss of something that we become aware of having had it to begin with. So for the little girl who loses the future expectation of "mothering" the taste of what was lingers on, and consequently women live in search of that contact, that care from their partner. Paradoxically because men in a sense haven't lost "it" they don't know "it" exists. So when a man says to his lover, "I don't know what it is you want that you're not getting," he means it. He doesn't really know what he's supposed to be giving that he isn't giving. For the woman it often is terribly difficult to put into words what it is she feels he's not giving. She wants to be listened to, deeply, respectfully, seriously. She wants him to be attentive to her, to care about what is going on inside of her emotionally. She wants care and concern and backup in the world. She wants the "woman" behind her in her life, supporting her success and development, and being both a consistent partner for her autonomy and self-hood—the same "woman" he has always had. Part of men's confusion about "what *do* women want?" is symptomatic of their own experience and what they've been able to take for granted.

But what we see is that "it"—the ability to listen, to care, to nurture, to relate intimately, to be emotional—is not just there by nature or magic. It is there because our society raises girls to provide it. Mothers teach their daughters to provide nurturance just as did their mothers before them. Mothers have been able to transmit to their sons something quite different. Because their sons are not like them, because they know their sons will not become women, wives, mothers, like themselves, mothers relate to their sons with a range of conscious and unconscious ideas about what it means to be a man. Boys come to experience emotional nurturing as part of the fabric of life. It is one of those invisible "laws" of patriarchal culture. Boys' and men's emotional dependency needs are less exposed and more continually met than those of women. Indeed part of the reason they are less exposed than women's is precisely because they are met on a more regular basis. Men usually do not have to crave emotional attention and connection because they receive it. They are given it by women who have been raised from their earliest days to supply it; to look to see what men are feeling, thinking, needing. Boys are not raised to develop the emotional antennae which girls acquire.

Men need women. Men search for women to care for them and love them. Men who are not in relationships and who want to be are extremely lonely, upset, in pain —just as are women in a similar situation. The point we are attempting to uncover is the myth that men are independent. That is one of the myths of patriarchy that must be examined and challenged. Men and women alike suffer from that myth. It makes everyone feel sick inside because they know themselves to be dependent and yet this very human emotion has been cast in such a bad light. In the next chapter we will look at the interplay between men and women in the fundamental dynamic of dependency.

■■■
❖ ❖ ❖

The Cha-Cha Phenomenon: Identifying Dependency Dynamics in Couples

Our emotions and our personalities reflect the culture in which we live. In our culture emotions are privatized. Most people feel that they know themselves or have an internal experience of themselves that no one else can know or see. Emotions are seen to be individual, subjective, personal. The extent to which culture shapes and delineates our emotions is obscured.[1]

It is within the adult intimate couple and the family that some degree of this isolation of emotional life is broken. As human beings we feel things all the time. It is not that there are specific times when we have emotional experiences. Yet, we learn how to not feel, how to

[1] The translucent boundary between the individual and society, the interrelatedness of the two, the ways in which our psychologies internalize the culture are not clear. In fact, dominant ideology in our culture is reflected in theories of psychology that emphasize that so much of what makes up our psychologies is instinctual. This ideology obscures the fact that people shape and create their society. It seems as if society has a life of its own, divorced from the people who make it up. And that the psychology of the people is divorced from the society.

control our feelings, and how to and when to express
ourselves emotionally. Much of this expression of emotion is relegated to the family. In our everyday experiences, whether at the market, at work, at school, or
dealing with bureaucracies, our feelings are aroused but
we don't vent them. We manage to keep our feelings to
ourselves. It is at home, in what is felt to be a safe and
private place, that we let ourselves feel much of what we
store up all day long. So, for example, a shoe salesman
who feels frustrated and angry after a hectic Saturday
will not blow his top at the job. He will probably let it
all out when he gets home, either with a long tirade
about all the people who drove him "mad" or by expressing his frustration and irritation more indirectly at
his wife or kids. The family is the place where strong
feelings are let out and expressed, where one gets some
emotional sustenance and relief.

The family as we know it is made up of a heterosexual
couple[2] and their children. The couple is the model for
adult intimate relationships.[3] Friends, work mates, col-
leagues, mothers, fathers, brothers, sisters, other relatives, neighbors all have a part in our social and emotional lives, but it is within the couple relationship that
deep levels of intimacy are sought and seem most possible. Our emotional vulnerabilities, our needs for love,
caring, and attention are brought to our partner in quite
a different way from other relationships.

The couple today is under enormous stress. Historically the husband and wife shouldered the hardships
of daily life together in a network of familial relationships. The extended family offered support. This is less
true today. The strains and stresses of our modern society bring with them new difficulties. When nuclear
war threatens us as a reality, when unemployment grows
to devastating proportions, the family suffers the im-

[2] We will discuss new forms of families—for example, gay couples,
communal groups, etc.—in chapter VII.
[3] For discussion of friends and how the couple as model affects friendships, see chapter VI.

pact of these social traumas. Living in a society that increasingly fails to meet the needs of the majority of its citizens creates a situation in which emotions are taut, people are on edge. Because our emotions are so privatized and because we experience so much emotional deprivation in many areas of our lives there is an enormous amount of need brought to the couple relationship. It is the family, and more specifically the adult couple within the family, in which so much of our social frustration and dissatisfaction get expressed. The changing roles of men and women, both economically and purposefully, brought about by the women's liberation movement mean that sexual politics and the power relations in the couple are currently being challenged. The old "man and wife" patterns are under scrutiny. The rules the modern couple can rely on are less clear. The couple flounders to find its feet.

The notion of a partner for life, someone with whom we can share our lives, is introduced to us from the moment of birth. The very process of becoming a person in our culture separates the inside experience of our emotions from the world outside of the boundaries of our bodies. As infants we experienced emotional and physical unity with mother—the inside and outside were all one. In the early period of psychological development, where we begin to develop a sense of ourselves as separate people and become aware of things around us, we enter into a culture that radically divides emotional life and the self from the society. We become aware of ourselves as separate entities within culture at the same time as we lose the sense of ourselves as being one with, related to, integrally bound up with our environment. We experience a split between our private and public worlds. There is then a further split within the private world (our psyches). Some of our private (internal) experiences become repressed and unconsciously we long to connect with a partner who will meet us in both worlds. Growing up we learn how to experience and express our emotions in particular ways. We learn how to "appropriately" respond to things that happen to us. We learn how to hold onto our emotional responses and to keep them inside—how to control ourselves. We learn these things by receiving unspoken messages from those around us who transmit a specific way of being within our particular culture. After all, they have grown up within that same culture and have embodied the form that they then transmit, thereby reproducing the next generation in that society. As children we watch our parents' relationship. We take in what we witness and develop expectations of what awaits us.

We develop hopes, fantasies, and expectations that one day, we, too, will have a partner, someone with whom we can share a special intimacy. Someone with whom to bridge these two worlds. Children's games reflect these hopes. We read about princes and princesses who at long last meet and live happily ever after. Even where a child grows up with parents who fight frequently and are unhappy in their marriage, expectations of a future coupling are shaped. Some parents may transmit to their children that they married the "wrong" person, that they are unhappy because of the other person. This does not necessarily stop the child's later desire and search for a partner. The child may come to feel that if she or he finds the "right" person it will all be different. Their ability for trust and intimacy will be skewed in particular ways but the model of the couple will still be ruling their visions. The norm in our society is the heterosexual couple, and anyone standing outside of that norm suffers social ostracism.

Dependency needs are brought into couple relationships in conscious and unconscious ways. While people want closeness and intimacy it is not always easy to achieve. In earlier chapters we have shown the ways in which women and men each look to intimate relationships with all kinds of conscious and unconscious expectations. Women and men look to a partner and a couple relationship in essential ways to shape their lives. Divorce rates have steadily risen and fewer and fewer couples stay together for a lifetime. Couples become aware of their frustrations and dissatisfactions and end relationships after several years, only to begin new ones. This is true nowadays even when there are children involved. Women and men in their thirties and forties today know that in the search for a new partner it is probable that there will be children involved. While divorce with children did occur thirty years ago, the frequency and "normality" of it have changed drastically.

And yet the high divorce rate does not prove that people no longer believe in marriage. The rate or remarriage is also high. After the pain of separation, women and men continue the search for a new partner, a partner who will better meet their needs and make them happy. People have a need for intimacy and emotional contact.

THE CHA-CHA PHENOMENON

It's Saturday afternoon. Janie and Peter are sitting in their living room reading. Janie looks over to Peter and feels waves of love for him. She loves the way he looks. She feels happy. She goes to sit next to him on the sofa, gives him a kiss. He looks up and smiles and looks back down at his book. Janie says, "Maybe we should forget about going to the movies tonight and just make a nice dinner at home. We can open our good wine." Peter responds, "Well, I really do feel like seeing that movie."

This is step one of the cha-cha. Janie feels open to Peter. She makes several gestures toward him for contact. The first rebuff was Peter looking down at the book after the kiss. The second move away from intimate contact was his rejection of the dinner-in idea. Janie felt both of these gestures as rejection.

Step two of the cha-cha:

Janie gets up and moves back to her chair. She feels hurt. She has a twinge of anger. She goes back to reading her book. In the silence of their reading there is a slight "chill" in the air between them. Janie does not look over to Peter and no longer feels filled with loving feelings as she did earlier.

Step three of the cha-cha:

Peter looks up from his book, yawns and stretches and looks over toward Janie. She doesn't look up, despite the sounds made from his yawn. He says, "Would you like a cup of coffee?"

Janie, still reading her book, says, "No, thanks." Peter goes into the kitchen, makes the coffee. Calls to Janie from the kitchen, "When do you think you'll want lunch, hon?" Janie: "Not yet." Peter comes back into the living room, goes over to Janie and gives her a kiss on the head. He sits himself on the arm of her chair and puts his arm around Janie. She looks up from her book, but not at Peter.

Peter becomes aware of the space between them that Janie's backing away in step two created. Feeling the space Peter moves toward Janie. There are now two possibilities for the next step.

Possibility one: Janie, after a minute or two, looks at Peter, takes his hand, and "comes back" to him. At this point the cha-cha is over. Perhaps Janie expresses some anger toward Peter and tells him that she felt hurt by his not wanting to stay in for the evening or by his pushing away when she approached him earlier on the couch. Or she may remain quiet and "let go" of the hurt and anger and respond to Peter.

Possibility two: Janie continues to look at her book and through her silence and ignoring of Peter lets him know that she is angry. He gets up from the arm of the chair and goes back to the couch and picks up his book, making a heavy sigh as he does this. They remain silent and the feeling in the room is chilly and uncomfortable for both of them. The cha-cha continues. At some point one of them will approach the other, and if there is a positive response the cha-cha will end. If, on the other hand, the response is tentative or cold, it is likely that the approaching partner will back off once again only to wait for the other to make the next move. The cha-cha continues.

This particular dynamic that happens within a couple relationship appears in several different forms. The basic dynamic involves one partner positively approaching the other in the pursuit of contact and the other retreating. Because of this to-ing and fro-ing we have come to call this the cha-cha phenomenon. One person in the couple feels loving, wants contact and closeness, makes moves toward her or his partner and is met with a rebuff, a distancing gesture. The reaction to this kind of rejection usually is a backing off, a retreat by the partner who originally approached. This is followed by a period of time (often quite brief) in which both partners feel distant, followed by the original "backing away" partner moving toward the other in an effort to retrieve her or him. The cha-cha phenomenon can occur with one partner (partner A) regularly being the approaching one and partner B regularly being the retreating or distancing one. It can occur with long intervals between the shift from who is doing the approaching and who is doing the backing off (several days or weeks). It can occur in an even balance between steps toward and steps away and which partner is doing what step at what point.

Also varying within the cha-cha phenomenon is the length of time the couple can sustain closeness and openness before one thing or another creates distance between them. It can take place in dramatic and explicit ways and in ways more subtle.

The cha-cha phenomenon is one way in which couples display a fear of intimacy. It is as if being close and loving for too long places one in jeopardy. One partner has to disentangle and back away. The cha-cha comes as an interruption of the intimacy. The reader may be thinking, "Just because Peter didn't want to stay in that night doesn't prove that he was retreating from intimacy. The guy just wanted to see a movie." We'll tell you a bit more about Janie and Peter so that we can see that cha-cha within the context of their relationship and the dependency/intimacy issues they were struggling with.

Just around the time of the sofa incident Janie and Peter had talked in couple counseling about a related problem. Peter felt that Janie was too dependent on him. He didn't like it that she needed him so much. He felt that she was too clinging and controlling. She organized their social plans and always seemed to him to be overly involved in the details and activities of his life. Janie, on the other hand, felt that Peter was often "absent" emotionally. That he was unaware of and forgetful about these things. She felt that he didn't really take care of them himself so she had to pick up the pieces.

Because Peter felt taken over or controlled by Janie he distanced himself by creating boundaries in order to keep her out. Each time he distanced himself more Janie reacted to his distancing by trying to move closer. Each time she moved closer Peter felt that she was taking him over and he would move further away in an attempt to preserve himself. Each time he moved further and strengthened the boundaries between them Janie felt this to be his being "absent" and unaware of things around him in their lives together. Janie's moving toward Peter in an attempt to get through his boundaries and Peter's retreating further and further in an attempt to escape what he unconsciously felt to be Janie's intention to possess him were a central feature of their relationship. The cha-cha phenomenon was just one of the outcomes. Only when Peter felt Janie to be distant from him, only when he felt the space and distance between them because she had backed away (emotionally), could he move toward her. Only when she was angry with him or hurt and withdrawn could he feel his feelings and need for her. Then he could come toward Janie.

The cha-cha phenomenon works to keep an emotional distance between a couple. It adds an element of precariousness to a couple's life together, it makes both members somewhat on edge and dissatisfied and yet it is so very prevalent. Could this be because it keeps each of us from confronting the very complicated feelings of fear of intimacy that are hard to put into words? If it is hard to face that phenomenon straight on, then the cha-cha, while distancing, has a function in keeping each member of the couple distanced enough to avoid that deeper fear.

Related to the dependency transactions within the cha-cha dynamics was Peter's repression of his own dependency needs when Janie was in pursuit of him. Janie carried the dependency in the relationship. Peter was afraid of his dependency feelings. It was very difficult for him to negotiate feeling his need for Janie and then not feeling swamped by her in his vulnerability. In therapy it emerged that Peter loved and needed Janie very much. His distancing and aloof behavior were a defense against his feelings of dependency. Janie's dependency and apparent clinging behavior served an important function in the relationship. As long as Janie held on firm to Peter and was overly involved with him, he did not feel at all insecure. His own dependency needs were being met "surreptitiously" by Janie appearing to need him so desperately. After all, if Janie was so dependent on Peter she would never leave. He felt very secure.

This illustrates another central feature of dependency and its relation to intimacy. That is something we call *carrying the dependency*. Peter's desire to come to couple therapy was extremely positive because unconsciously he knew that he needed Janie to back off, or let go a bit, in order for him to emotionally be in the relationship. He knew that emotionally he was going further and further away and couldn't help himself even though he knew he didn't want to. In therapy we discovered reasons why Peter had come to feel that a woman could take him over, or possess him, and why he felt he had to create such firm boundaries between himself and his partner. Much of this had to do with his early childrearing and his relationship to his mother. In therapy he was able to expose his dependency needs and to feel that Janie wouldn't swallow him up because of this. As Peter became less defensive and able to show his love more and to sustain close contact for longer periods of time, Janie's clinging behavior diminished. Because she no longer felt pushed away by Peter and was able to feel more secure in his love for her, she was able to be more autonomous. She felt freer to make plans that didn't involve Peter and she had more trust that Peter was handling his own emotional affairs. She now felt that he was aware of his emotions and could maintain his own social contacts and no longer undermined him in these areas.

Within the couple relationship, the dissolution of barriers, the intimacy, and the longing for closeness bring their own problems. Beginnings of relationships often seem so easy. There is usually terrific excitement, fluttery feelings, eagerness for sexual contact, lots of things to talk about with one another, desire to please the other by the way we dress, cook a meal, display attentiveness, etc. These beginnings at "getting connected" seem almost effortless. For some couples, as time goes by, the sexual relationship and the channels of emotional understanding and communication get stronger and better. For many couples the love between two people grows and the connection deepens. For all couples there is some degree of friction and struggle. Disappointments and flare-ups happen as quickly as a flash of lightning, often for no apparent reason. Mood changes are affected dramatically and instantaneously. People unwittingly have impulses to control or direct their partner. Partners withdraw from each other emotionally and physically, only to return again to closeness. Many couples feel that as time goes by they have less to talk about than they did in the beginning years or they feel their sexual interest has diminished.

This brings us to a question that must be addressed. That is, if people so obviously need and search for contact and emotional intimacy why is it that achieving this intimacy is at times so difficult or, more to the point, why is it that once we achieve a certain level of intimacy it is so difficult to sustain?

The fear of intimacy is a very common but unrecognized phenomenon. Although there does seem to be a pattern that many relationships follow, we must, of course, note that there are innumerable nuances within each couple, depending upon the psychology of each partner. Most people are not aware or conscious of their fear of intimacy. It shows up in different ways. The majority of relational difficulties have an element of the fear of intimacy in them. The fear of intimacy is woven by many threads: the divorce between the public and private world; the psychological phenomenon of transference; the narcissistic needs out of which we seek to relate; the narcissistic gratifications we crave in another. All these phenomena are created in the context of our parenting and child-raising arrangements, which bring particular pressures to our first love affair—the love we all experienced with our mothers, the blueprint for all our close relationships.

The first and most intimate relationship both women and men have is with mother. Not only do we come from her body, where we were merged with her, but our psychological merger with mother carried on into the first year of our lives. In previous chapters we have explained the way in which an infant, before developing a sense of self, is merged with mother. That is, the infant feels mother in his or her world; there are no boundaries and everything that comes into the infant's world feels in some sense as if it is a part of the infant himself or herself. All of the early experiences of eating and taking in mother's milk, feeling the warmth and comfort and satisfaction of that experience, are not erased from our memories. They become part of us. Similarly all of the unpleasant and frightening experiences of hunger, pain, discomfort, yearning for contact, and the familiar smell and touch that is not there at the moment the infant is wanting it—all of these upsets and fears are repressed or forgotten, but not erased from our psyches.

As adults there are certain experiences that generate feelings we had in infancy. Some experiences resonate on a visceral level or vaguely remind us of something we can't put our fingers on, something we can't quite remember why it is familiar or why we feel we've experienced it before. Yet what actually may be happening is that a deeply buried or forgotten memory is being touched, stirred.

Deep intimacy in adult relationships seems to touch many of the unconscious memories we have of our early, intimate relationship with mother. In that relationship she was very big and extremely powerful in relation to us. We were dependent on her for our survival. She seemed to have a magical power in which she could either make the world safe and satisfying and deliciously cozy or the power to create a terrorizing, empty, frightening world where we feared for our very survival. As we developed we took in her caring and loving (as well as that of others) and we developed capabilities for becoming more autonomous. As toddlers growing and separating from mother, we became less dependent in certain ways. We began to put spoons into our own mouths; we began to walk, enabling us to get places without being carried, etc. Each step was a step that took us further from that original merger and utter dependency.

This is the stuff of which the fear of dependency is made. In our developing emotional and physical intimacy with a lover various dynamics take place that resonate at a psychological level with that early experience of merger and dependency. People have an unconscious fear that in their closeness in adult relationships, they will lose themselves, that they will return to that early state where they were actually one with their partner and in the merger will be swallowed up and lost. Unconsciously they fear that they will not regain their sense of themselves as separate from their partner. A commitment and deep connection with another stir feelings of utter contentment, bliss, and unity as well as feelings of being confined, restrained, imprisoned. For some people the negative aspects of the early merger that are recalled are so disturbing and unmanageable that they feel better when they are not in a relationship. They have a different experience of themselves, perhaps freer.

Let's take a closer look at some of the ways in which people protect themselves from this fear of intimacy.

Janet and Laurie met at a women's bar. They became lovers and for several weeks spent almost twenty-four hours a day together. They enjoyed one another thoroughly and from the beginning felt a strong compatibility. Janet began to stay at Laurie's apartment four or five nights a week. On the days Janet intended to go back to her own apartment after work Laurie, for one reason or another, would be withdrawn, perhaps irritated, generally in some kind of a bad mood. They would leave each other feeling a bit distant. Even when they had had an especially lovely and close time together on the preceding days, inevitably they would part with less than warm and loving feelings. This escalated to the point where they would actually have arguments on the mornings that Janet was going back to her place. The pattern that followed was that for that night they each, in their own apartments, would feel terrible and somewhat angry with the other, then the following day one would call the other, they would make plans to get together either that night or the next and after being together for a couple of chilly hours, they eventually warmed up and had a loving and intimate time together. This would continue for the two or three days they stayed together and then the same pattern would repeat itself all over again when Janet was leaving. When they finally talked about it, what emerged was that Laurie wanted them to live together and each time that Janet went home Laurie took this as a sign that Janet didn't want to be with her as much as she wanted to be with Janet. Laurie felt rejected and hurt and this was why she withdrew and acted annoyed. She was trying to protect herself from Janet's leaving by "leaving" first.

In subtle ways Laurie carried the dependency feelings in the relationship. Janet was able to come and go because Laurie's dependency needs provided the base, the anchor that helped Janet to feel very secure, loved and wanted within the relationship. With those secure feelings she was able to be away from Laurie and be involved in other aspects of her life, such as her work, her political meetings, etc.

In Laurie and Janet's relationship there was both a physical withdrawing—for example, Janet going to her apartment—and an emotional withdrawing—Laurie withdrawing herself emotionally, becoming distant and irritated with Janet on the mornings she left. The "chilly" hours spent when they got back together was the time they both had to renegotiate the emotional and physical coming together again. It took a bit of time for Laurie to come out of herself and to open up to Janet, to let her be close again emotionally. This couple thoroughly enjoyed their intimacy when they were together and open. The difficulties they experienced were around being apart. But, in another respect, Laurie always felt powerless in relation to Janet. She felt at Janet's mercy. Janet seemed to have control over the comings and goings and Laurie was emotionally on a see-saw, always being ready to prepare herself for the "loss" of Janet. Janet seemed to be able to handle the brief separations without any difficulty. She seemed to stay intact throughout while Laurie felt emotional waves of invasion and loss. Psychologically Janet held the firm boundaries while Laurie held the needs.

It often appears that one partner in a couple is more dependent than the other partner. More often these seem to be fixed positions, but there are times when this position in relation to the dependency may shift back and forth. For the majority of couples it is the woman who appears to be the dependent one. Women are thought to be more "clingy," needy, and helpless. Women's emotional lives often seem to be much more caught up in their relationships than do men's. Men often appear more independent and secure within their relationships. In chapter II we showed the ways in which men's dependency needs are often hidden from view because of their psychological development and their socialization to a male role. We showed the ways in which boys continue to receive maternal nurturance and do not have to give up their mother or their expectation of continued emotional nurturance and how this, in turn, makes them less emotionally hungry than women. Their dependency need may not appear as great because it is more regularly satisfied and fed. In chapter I we showed that this experience is not parallel for girls, because they must give up their expectation of continued maternal nurturance in order to become heterosexual women in our society. We explained how girls come to feel deprived and hungry emotionally; how they come to feel that there is something wrong with them (in order to justify why they were pushed away by mother); how they come to feel as if their emotional needs are overwhelming and fear that perhaps there is an unending well of neediness inside, which they must hide.

Because women come not to expect satisfactory emotional nurturance and understanding from their partners, men's inadequacy in giving this nurturance is to some extent accepted and even anticipated by women. In the beginning of a relationship, because of the heightened emotional activity that is a part of the courting process, the promise of a nurturant partner looks hopeful. As time goes on and men's attentiveness wanes, women feel tremendous loss and disappointment. Women often express great disdain for men's ignorance in emotional matters. This contempt is rarely expressed directly. When women do express their needs it often comes out as a criticism. When a woman feels disappointments or the lack of emotional attention and care she so desperately wants there is a buildup of emotional upset, because while she may accept that she won't get it, she fights this knowledge because she still feels such great need. The woman may declare that she doesn't feel happy in the relationship, that he doesn't give enough emotionally, and so on. He wants her to be more specific, because he doesn't know what she's talking about. He responds to the criticism with anger, which frightens her. She finds it hard to be more specific. She wonders why he doesn't know what she means. How come he doesn't understand this? She understands and intuits what he feels even when he doesn't put it perfectly into words, and so on. She also begins to feel shaky because her most feared fantasy is actually happening. She is being pushed away and rejected because her needs are exposed. She hears him say that she's too needy, that he doesn't know what she wants, that no matter what he does it's never right, and she feels this to be true too. The fight is often resolved in the following way. She cries and backs off, taking the bad feelings into herself, feeling that once again her anger was impotent. She feels defeated and in despair, thinking she will never get what she needs and that it's just as much her fault as his because she doesn't even know what it is she wants. He gives her a hug and kiss, and as he does this she feels better. They make up. Until next time. He feels relieved that it's over and that it all had to do with her overneediness and really did not have much to do with his behavior. He may have a slight twinge of guilt, although it feels diffuse and he can't really pinpoint what it's about. He may feel unhappy that she was so upset. But the psychological fit is that the woman feels her needs are too great, and so the defenses that the man has constructed against his own feelings of inadequacy in the arena of emotional nurturance and the defenses against feeling his "femininity" seem necessary because of what appears to be the woman's insatiability. It is not seen as his not knowing how to give adequately, but rather that she wants too much. The woman's psychology prepares her to collude in this dynamic and to protect her man from these feelings of inadequacy. She does not want to expose his "weakness" and vulnerability because then she loses the illusion of this being the person who can love and take care of her. She looked for someone to "replace" her mother; she hoped that she finally found a person who would love and care for her again, and therefore she joins with him in hiding from view the fact that he may not be able to provide this nurturance. If she exposes that he can't then she feels bereft and alone once again.

The man who is unconsciously trying to repress his "femininity" and his early connection to mother (his being like her) cannot afford psychologically to have his woman trying to expose that part of him. *Psychologically the man is in a terrible bind. On the one hand he must repress this aspect of his personality* (which has been stifled from development) *in order to be a man, and at the same time, in a loving relationship, he must tap this part of himself and draw on it.* In order for a man to give the emotional contact a woman wants, he is involved in a process that directly threatens his conception of self.

Ilene and Thomas were married for twenty-three years. When they first met they thought the world of each other. Ilene, who had not had a very loving family background, felt that at long last she had someone to really love her. Thomas was handsome and charming, he had a growing business and he treated Ilene gallantly. She worshipped him and was utterly devoted. Over the years of their marriage Ilene catered to Thomas's desires, trying to be a superwife. She decorated the house elegantly, prepared gourmet dishes for dinner, worked at keeping her body trim and pleasing to Thomas, and was hostess to his business affairs. They had two children. When Thomas went away on business trips Ilene wanted him to call her each day. She felt she needed that contact and wanted to know that he was all right. When she would ask him questions about these small trips he would get irritated. He wanted to know why she wanted to know these things, why she was always having to involve herself in all aspects of his life? Ilene felt rejected and upset; she began to feel that Thomas was hiding something from her. She began to feel suspicious about where he was whenever he was away from her. She asked his secretary lots of questions about his luncheon dates and business meetings. She felt herself becoming more and more insecure, nervous, and clingy. She couldn't imagine what she would ever do without Thomas; he was her life; she lived for him. She continually vowed to herself not to ask Thomas questions about who was at the meeting, where it was being held, etc. Each time she did he became furious with her and yet each time it seemed to slip out of her before she could catch herself. During an argument that followed one of these exchanges Thomas told Ilene "not to push him." She was frightened. What did he mean by that? Was he planning on leaving her? She had better be careful and keep her upset to herself and act like everything was fine, loosen the reins, not ask questions.

One evening Ilene's friend Roseann saw Thomas at a restaurant with a woman. She told Ilene about it. Ilene's world collapsed. This is what she had suspected for some months; this is what she had been trying to find out from Thomas and now she finally knew. When he came home that evening she confronted him with the information. He said that it was true and that he wanted to stay with Ilene but he wouldn't stop seeing the other woman, because they had become too involved. Ilene said that she couldn't live like that, and after much pain and anger they decided to separate.

For the next six months Ilene suffered terribly. She felt herself lost at the bottom of the sea. Her children, now twenty and sixteen, felt sorry for her and angry with their father. Then Ilene woke up one day and decided that she couldn't continue to live in the house they had shared for so many years. She was starting to feel better; she had to continue her life and she had to move herself out of Thomas's surroundings. She found a lovely apartment and moved in. She decorated it just the way she liked and actually had moments of exuberance and joy about what she was creating. Meanwhile, the children saw their father irregularly, but each time they saw him they reported on how Ilene was doing. In the period when Ilene was feeling stronger and developing her own life apart from Thomas, he decided to visit her. Ilene was shocked to see Thomas. She felt quite shaken but tried very hard not to show this to him. She showed him the apartment and talked about the various things she had done to fix it up. She told him how she was beginning to look for work. Thomas felt himself attracted to Ilene. When he left he felt shaken up and upset. Over the next few days he thought about Ilene often. He wanted to see her again. It wasn't until Ilene appeared not to need him that he became aware of the fact that he hadn't let go of her in his own mind, that over the period of the separation, somewhere in the back of his mind he still felt that Ilene was there. He felt that she needed him so badly that he could always go back to her. As she began to separate from him emotionally and turn her energies toward herself and outward, he became frightened and aware of his own dependency on Ilene.

In all years of their marriage Ilene appeared to be the dependent partner. She held firmly to Thomas and because she held firmly he felt secure. This fit together with his upbringing, which informed him that as a man he should not be dependent, that dependency, meant weakness. In effect, Thomas did not feel his own dependency needs. All the ways in which he depended on Ilene—for his daily care, for her listening and concern, for her support of his success, for her raising his children, for her providing him with sexual pleasure and satisfaction, for her caring for his home, his clothes— were hidden and taken for granted. To everyone, including Ilene and Thomas, it looked as if she was the dependent partner. It wasn't until Ilene began to really separate from Thomas, eight months after the physical separation, that he was forced to feel his dependency. Up until that point, even in their physical separation, he still emotionally needed to feel that Ilene was there for him.

Thomas exemplifies the benefits men get in a patriarchal society as well as the damage and impairment. We can look at Thomas's life and see that he was catered to and respected and looked up to and looked after in ways that gave him the status of king in his own home. He was a successful man. His emotional and physical dependency needs continued to be met. Being raised as a man Thomas unconsciously came to expect much of this, and so had little difficulty in accepting all of his luxurious attention. He felt he deserved it and he took it all in without psychic difficulty. Thomas's impairment was his inability to feel or show himself as emotionally vulnerable. Thomas could not feel love easily. His emotions were tied up inside him. Showing love, feeling dependency, and vulnerability felt to him as great weakness. His emotions felt infantile to him; they made him feel small. He could not tolerate these feelings. They left him feeling far too vulnerable and fragile. He needed Ilene to carry all of the dependency in the relationship because he could not afford to exhibit any of his own. Emotions felt feminine and Thomas was a man.

Dependency and intimacy are closely connected. Closeness and contact with another may make one feel vulnerable. Many people have difficulty in showing their love or affection because they feel too vulnerable and worry that they may be rejected or thought to be silly. People often keep their feelings of love inside in an attempt to protect themselves from anticipated hurt and rejection. We have the ability to create invisible barriers between ourselves and others. Sometimes we feel we have control over the raising and lowering of these barriers. Often these barriers feel like they have wills of their own and even though we may want to say, "I love you," or we may want to take our lover's hand in ours, we feel paralyzed. The barriers not only keep the other person out but they also hold us back. We can be imprisoned by our boundaries, which keep us from achieving the intimacy we long for.

Showing love, exposing our need and desire for contact, touches our feelings of dependency. Letting ourselves feel our wants for another person is a kind of letting go. It is letting ourselves be open and vulnerable to another person. It is a giving of ourselves. Emotional dependency, needing, wanting, and giving love to another person, is the fabric of intimate relationships. In the realm of our emotional lives people are both strong and sensitive. Loving someone and feeling emotionally vulnerable to them is both effortless and painstaking. It is the easiest thing in the world and the most difficult. We long for intimacy and we fear intimacy.

When we are involved in a relationship our emotional channel is on fine-tuning. We feel disappointments for the smallest occurrences. We are so psychologically tuned in to our partners that their behavior or even their mood affects the way we ourselves feel. Let's take a step back to the beginning of a relationship to find what creates the fine-tuning in intimate relationships.

FALLING IN LOVE

What attracts two people to each other? Why do certain physical types attract certain people and other physical types attract others? Are there matches "made in heaven"? Upon first meeting one sees only a handful of things about another person. We see the way a person is dressed, what her or his face looks like, the physical presence. Many people find themselves drawn to a particular physical type, be it tall, short, thin, stocky, long-haired, fair-haired, dark, etc. When people meet there is usually some aspect that attracts one to another. If the attraction is mutual there is a spark and contact is made. At the very beginning of a relationship two people actually know very little about each other. The process of getting to know someone is an intricate one. In a relatively short time one can learn about someone else's background, family, class, education, where that person grew up, what her or his occupation is and so on. It takes quite a lot longer, however, to begin to get to *know* another person more intimately, that is, how another person thinks and feels about things. It takes time to become familiar, to get to know what the person is like inside, to know that part that others rarely see. It takes time to reach the fine-tuning of communication and exchange. On a daily basis, deeper understanding takes place in relating.

Although it takes time to develop intimacy it is the exception rather than the rule today that two people who are attracted to each other take time to get to know the other and then "fall in love." Most often people seem to "fall in love" early in the relationship and get to know each other after. Indeed, it might be said that falling in love is the first step required in pursuing a relationship. There are some couples who have known each other for a number of years,[4] perhaps they have been friends and eventually become lovers, so that the falling in love happens after the knowing.

Hollywood has filled our minds and hearts with images of love at first sight. Two people spot each other across a crowded room and their eyes meet. Music streams from the heavens, filling us all with the magic of the moment. Countless couples over the decades have found each other on the screen and at that powerful moment we all feel that this is what we, too, have been waiting for. Fred Astaire and Ginger Rogers have at last found the partner they have been waiting for—the answer to their dreams and the resolution to their lives.

[4] For historic changes discussed in sex and dependency see chapter IV.

They glide across the floor together, perfectly in step and filled with the joy that this is the best that life offers.

At the risk of destroying the mystique that surrounds falling in love or bursting the bubble of romance we'd like to take a closer look at this phenomenon of falling in love. Indeed, there are many levels to the attraction of two people to each other, some which actually have to do with the qualities we see in the other person and some which have more to do with our own psychology and who we need the other person to be. Various psychological dynamics, such as narcissistic needs, narcissistic identification, and transference may at any point be a part of the relating process.

Narcissistic Needs

Alison meets Jack at a party. She is attracted to him. She thinks that he is a great dancer and very good looking. He has dark eyes, which she notices immediately. He smiles at her and they begin to talk. Jack is comfortable and friendly. He seems very at ease with himself and appears to be a gentle person. Alison feels herself falling in love. In bed that night Alison can't stop thinking about Jack. She imagines him meeting her friends and family and being very charming and everyone loving him. She feels she could be with him forever.

Alison doesn't know Jack. They spent all of twenty minutes talking to each other at the party. How do we explain the fantasies that Alison had about her life together with Jack? Fantasy plays a big part in falling in love, because at the very beginning we have all of our needs and we are psychologically "ready" to have a person come along to fit in with and meet them. Fantasies are within our control. We can create them to soothe ourselves, stimulate ourselves, upset ourselves; we can create good endings and bad endings, we can create joyful moments and deeply distressing ones. Alison felt a part of her to be empty inside. Although she had friends and family who cared about her, she had an unsettled feeling deep within. Jack was warm and friendly and gentle. Alison's brief interaction with Jack and her experience of these qualities in his personality evoked her yearning and hope that here was a person who could meet her needs. Our needs affect our vision of who a person might be. In the forefront of Alison's fantasies were her needs and longings and in the background were the particulars of who Jack actually was. Somewhere along the line in Alison's early psychological development she did not secure and internalize a firm sense of self. She looked to another person, Jack, to complete her sense of self. She wanted him out of her own emptiness. She was relating out of a narcissistic need.

Another example of a narcissistic need is one person wanting contact with another because of a characteristic that other person possesses that she or he feels is missing in herself or himself. So, for example, Daniel, an extremely introverted and shy man with tight boundaries, fell in love with Cynthia, who on the surface was extremely friendly, warm, and giving. She was always able to make people feel at ease and social situations were comfortable and easy for her. Through Daniel's relationship with Cynthia he was able to feel that he now possessed some of those qualities he lacked. Some of Cynthia's outgoingness seemed to rub off on him. He felt more secure in social situations when she was with him. In this relationship the narcissistic need actually worked both ways because Cynthia, in fact, was quite out of control and "all over the place." She did not feel a clear sense of boundaries. She found it impossible to say no, for example, and was so involved in other people's needs and wants that she was not "living in her own skin." In her relationship with Daniel, Cynthia unconsciously utilized his rigid boundaries for her own sense of containment.

Like Cynthia and Daniel, often couples seem to fit. What they see as complementary personalities are in fact more than that. They both respond out of unconscious needs to the attributes and psychological shape of the other's personality. It is astonishing to realize the power of unconscious processes in our search for and choice of a partner. The expression "a match made in heaven" describes a fit that works well. Two people come together, each with their own psychology, their own emotional history and development, their own needs and expectations and ability to be in a relationship. The intricacies of emotional energy that flows between an intimate couple are elaborate.

Narcissistic Identification

We all have aspects of our personalities that we like and those that we don't like. Sometimes we try to hide as best we can those aspects we think are unpleasant or ugly. One way of insuring that these aspects stay out of sight is to be connected to people who seem to have the attributes with which we prefer to identify. That is, we may like to be with people who seem to be the way we would like to be. In relationships we may choose partners who possess the characteristics we like in ourselves. We may like people because of the way they dress, the way they look, the kind of work they do, the way they think about things, their political perspectives, the kind of car they drive, their taste in food, their cultural interests, sports interests, etc. We wish to get closer to these people because we like all kinds of things about them. Often these things mirror aspects of ourselves that we like or they may represent the way we strive to be.

Narcissistic identifications in couples may emerge after a time in a relationship and become apparent when one partner suddenly feels upset or critical about an aspect of who the other partner is. Often it appears in quite trivial ways. For example, six months into their relationship Rena found herself disturbed by Al's bell-bottom trousers, which she found to be too wide and out of fashion. Every time they were together when he wore the wide bell-bottoms she found herself turned off and somewhat distant and irritated by him all evening. Rena's unconscious narcissistic identification with Al was such that she could not tolerate his looking any way that did not accurately reflect the way *she* wanted to look and wanted to be seen. Many people are extremely sensitive to the way others see and think about their partners. We may be concerned with the way our partner talks about various topics in a social situation—is he or she saying the right things, does everyone think this person is witty, weird, etc? We begin to see our partner as an extension of ourself. We feel as if we are being judged at the same time we imagine other people to be judging our partner.

In relationships people become psychologically merged. Many aspects of a couple's daily life represent merger. Setting up a place to live together, buying furniture to share are examples; other examples of merger include cooking and eating food together, sharing closets, towels, etc., and sharing money. (Money representing merger or separateness is very common. The ways couples deal with money can say an awful lot about the dynamics in their relationship.) In many ways it is an extremely pleasurable experience. It represents a letting go of a firmly fixed position of "mine." If one feels secure enough in oneself, then sharing and merger do not represent loss of self. They show that developmentally one has achieved a secure sense of selfhood and is able to move into the world of "mature" relationships. If a person feels this level of internal security, then she or he can tolerate more easily differences in her or his partner—even differences that she or he doesn't like. If, for example, your partner likes to eat red licorice in a roomful of friends who are gourmet cooks, you would be able to tolerate this. You won't feel the need to hide the licorice, or pray that your mate doesn't eat it there for fear that your friends will think badly of your partner and, therefore, think badly of you. In a couple relationship, the feeling of discomfort in the merger stems from the feeling that our partner is an extension of ourselves. We try to control ourselves in order to appear in a way we have come to think is acceptable. We then find ourselves trying to control our partner in order to have her or him also appear in acceptable ways.

In these times, when the world may seem less and less a safe place, we are thrown back on ourselves. Our individuality and our personal lives seem to be the only things we can even hope to have some control over. Through distorted lenses we meticulously observe ourselves to see that everything is in order. This phenomenon extends to the couple relationship where our lovers, as narcissistic extensions of ourselves, are also under the critical magnifying lens.

Transference

A person's emotional makeup greatly influences his or her choice of partners. People bring a whole range of unconscious expectations that were experienced in earlier relationships to adult relationships. This is what Freud called transference. He discovered in the analytic relationship that his patients were unconsciously acting toward him as if he were their father or mother. They expected him to act and react in ways that reproduced the ways in which a parent acted. This happens to a great extent in all kinds of relationships. It is often a revelation to a man married for several years suddenly to realize that his wife is just like his mother in central ways. It is even more shocking when a woman realizes that her husband is just like *her* mother in many ways!

In the beginning phase of a relationship the transference either works or it doesn't. Someone may have a negative transference, for instance, where they experience a partner's behavior resonating with the most dreaded characteristics of a parent, cutting the possibility of the continuation of that relationship.

For example, Janis met Robert at a bar. They chatted for a while and Robert asked to go out with Janis again.

The next time they went out Janis decided that she really didn't like him. She couldn't quite pinpoint why this was so, because as she described the evening it sounded quite nice. When Janis talked about this in her therapy and wondered why she didn't like him she found herself describing his joke-telling. She remarked that he had told many brief jokes over the evening and that although at the time she laughed, something about it bothered her. Her associations to this reminded her of the way in which her father tried to get people to laugh a lot of the time and how she often felt embarrassed by his behavior. She felt upset knowing that her father was needing the attention and was trying so desperately to be liked. She found it sad and it filled her with feelings of pity for him. She realized that the reason she didn't "go" for Robert was that she superimposed this same quality onto him, just because of the joke-telling. This is transference. In fact, Janis didn't know Robert well enough to have any idea what his joke-telling was about, but in his behaving in a way that reminded her of her father she unconsciously superimposed a whole set of other emotional characteristics onto him that were actually about her father's personality. Transference can get in the way of starting a relationship but it also operates to cement relationships in both healthy and unhealthy ways.

Rosemary and Neil have been together for ten years. Neither of them feels really good about the relationship. Although they manage to have some good times, for the most part they feel dissatisfied. And yet they stay together. Neil is very withholding and for almost all of the ten years has tried to maintain a certain position of privacy within the relationship. He responds to Rosemary's questions with irritation and annoyance, as if everything she asks is a demand. Emotionally and sexually he is very rejecting. In Rosemary's therapy she became aware of how, by living with Neil, she keeps reliving over and over again the rejections she felt from her mother. Rosemary lived with a continual feeling of deprivation and emotional hunger. She always felt as if things were her fault and that she wanted too much. She also felt as if there was something wrong with her, that she was undesirable, or else why didn't Neil and her mother love her more and give her more attention and care? Being related to in this way was so familiar to Rosemary that the prospect of things being different was actually quite scary. Holding on to the "bad" attention at some level felt safer than letting go of it. She didn't know what else could replace it. Being connected to her mother with all of the pain, hurt, and anger that came with it felt less frightening psychologically than breaking free of the connection. Rosemary's putting up with Neil's continual rejection was satisfying an unhealthy need. She was, in effect, still living with her mother.

Transference in relationships can cross sex. In Rosemary's case there was a mother transference in operation. The equation can include any number of possibilities—mother-daughter, father-daughter, mother-son, father-son. Sometimes one is drawn to an aspect of another that reminds her or him of a sister, a brother, an aunt or uncle, a nanny, or early childcare person other than mother. Transference can take many forms, for example, attraction to someone because of physical or personality traits that remind one of a father, mother, etc. The new partner may, indeed, have similar qualities, so the reader might ask, "Isn't it those real traits that the person is reacting to?" The significance of the transferential piece is all of the meaning and the range of feelings that one attributes to those particular traits. There can be a wealth of associations and expectations attached to a particular personality trait. For instance, Rebecca loves that Larry sings to her. When she was a little girl her mother used to sing to her and so she finds Larry's singing comforting. It is not just Larry singing in the present tense that fills Rebecca with warm and cozy feelings, which it does. It is the powerful resonance at a subconscious level that produces those feelings in her. The fact that Rebecca then unconsciously relates to Larry in many other ways as if he were her mother is all part of the transference operating in their relationship.

The fact that one's partner is *not* one's mother or father and therefore does *not* respond as she or he did creates the possibility of individuals changing and growing emotionally. You may feel pleasantly surprised by a response your partner had had to something you have done. The surprised feeling is the clue to the transference—the unconscious expectation that there would be a different response.

For example, when Rosa first started living with Bruce she noticed that when she missed the 5:30 P.M. train home from work and got home twenty minutes later because she caught the 6:00 P.M. train, she would feel anxious from 5:20 P.M. until the time she saw Bruce. At those times he would get home just before her at 6:15 P.M. Each time Bruce greeted her lovingly she felt relieved and thankful. She didn't know why this was. In thinking about this Rosa realized that as a girl whenever she came home from school even a few minutes later than expected or when she would be visiting a friend after school and got home a few minutes late for dinner her mother would be furious with her. She would be met at the door with anger and her mother would treat her coldly for several hours thereafter. Each time Bruce greeted her lovingly she was somewhat shocked. Because of the transference in their close relationship Rose unconsciously expected Bruce to react just as her mother had. After several months of living together Rosa's anxiety at missing the 5:30 train began to diminish. This particular dynamic affected other aspects of their relationship and of Rosa's psychology. There were many ways in which Bruce's less rigid expectations and controls and fears within the relationship (less than Rosa's mother) helped Rosa to relax and to be less hard on herself, less punishing.

Sometimes a person in a couple may unconsciously try to provoke her or his partner into responding just like father or mother did in the past. Getting a different reaction doesn't satisfy a deeply held conception. If one needs to "do battle" with a parent because as an adult one still feels left with all sorts of unfinished psychological business, then a way to make this happen is to do battle with the new partner.

For example, George saw a pattern to his fights with Marion. Each time Marion criticized him for being too selfish and unaware of ways in which he ignored or hurt her they would have a big argument. George says that at first he feels defensive because he is being accused of being "bad," but at the same time or just moments thereafter he feels guilty because he knows she is right. The yelling and screaming that follow in their fight ultimately has Marion telling George what an awful person he is. Marion meanwhile feels extremely upset about how ugly their fights get at these times. George began to sense that somehow he provoked Marion until he got the fight to that painful level. Marion's original criticism might have been terribly small and insignificant but George took it and blew it up into something that he knew had little to do with Marion. It had to do with himself. He wondered why he seemed to steer their fights in the same direction time and time again. In analyzing the transferential aspects of their relationship it became clear that George was fighting with Marion a continuing battle he had had with his father. When George was a boy, his father often made him feel that he had disappointed him. George would feel terribly ashamed and guilty. He developed a poor self-image. Deep inside he felt he was not good enough. He saw himself through his father's eyes and always fell short of what was expected of him. In his relationship with Marion, George unconsciously continued the battle with his father. Each time Marion said that she felt he didn't act properly, that triggered a well of feelings inside him. He brought their fights to terribly painful levels, where he would feel as if he was receiving a beating from Marion. He would be getting Marion to psychologically beat him because he was not good enough.

Falling in love and relating with someone are not just transference, narcissistic identification, or narcissistic need. In the beginning of an intimate relationship there are two people, each with their own unique psychology and history, who come together to enjoy, share, exchange, care, relate, experience each other. Having another person to whom one is attracted respond favorably (for whatever reasons) and reciprocate loving feelings can be a transforming experience. Receiving love and feeling and giving love, whether it comes from conscious or unconscious resources, are a human need and activity. In most relationships there is at least a thread of newness, a reaching outward in an attempt to connect to another person. Every relationship has aspects of it that can be seen as neurotic, but relationships are multidimensional. Even in what may appear to be the most unhealthy and neurotic of relationships when one scratches beneath the surface the need and desire for human contact are always there. If part of being human is about being connected, then intimate relating, however distorted, is an expression of this human need for contact.

Dependency in relationships also is multidimensional. In many ways just being in a couple engages dependency needs, regardless of how much care and emotional connectedness the two people may have. There are couples who, to a large extent, meet each other's dependency needs in more direct and equal ways. There are couples who remain married for a lifetime and truly share their lives with each other, including all of the struggles as well as the joys. But there are many couples for whom the very existence of the relationship is paramount. We saw in Rosemary's case that while she actually received little nurturing from Neil, on another level her dependency needs were being contained within the relationship. Her lack of psychological and emotional separation from her mother meant that there was still an aspect of her dependency needs that was shaped by an unsatisfactory situation. Her dependency need was met in form, by being married, even though the content of her needs was not. If the reader can remember back to chapter I, in Margaret and Robert's relationship there was a similar phenomenon. For so many years Margaret and Robert stayed together despite the daily dissatisfactions they each felt. Experiences and relationships that each of them had in their infancy and childhoods shaped their particular psychologies, and those psychologies enabled them to stay in that relationship for a lifetime. There was, so to speak, a fit.

Loving relationships are a complicated matrix of dependency, intimacy, psychological yearnings, and fears. In the next chapter we take a look at how these themes are expressed in the sexual aspects of intimate relationships.

IV

❖ ❖ ❖

Sex and Dependency

Our attitudes about sex and sexuality make for a complex and contradictory tapestry. So much of what we feel and think about sex is formed by prejudice of one kind or another. Often we aren't sure what we really believe. The subject touches raw nerves, running along emotional tributaries. Sometimes we are open and receptive, at other times inexplicably defensive. Daily we are bombarded by different images of sexuality. Sex is used to sell toothpaste, to cement marriage, to stem anxiety, to make babies, to provide reassurance, to show love, to exercise power. Sex is always linked with something else. If the object is inanimate, such as a car, the sexual association humanizes it, imbues it with sexual vitality. At the same time, sex itself becomes stripped of its humanity and appears as a commodity, a thing to be had.

It is easier to describe sex and sexuality as they appear within various forms than to strictly define them. The difficulty is compounded by the fact that our notion of sexuality is a changing one. In recent history we have become a prurient society. The attitudes we acquire about sex are imbued with a sense of the forbidden, of impurity and shame. We are curious and hesitant.

We enter a world of sexual relationships that we act upon but did not create. We are players in a script we see as unique and deeply personal. Sexuality is intimacy, the apex of individual expression. But we are the heirs of our parents' sexuality and inherit the values and norms of their generation.

Our parents' generation grew up with a more uniform view of sex. There were "good" women and there were "loose" women. Men were required to be "experienced" for their virgin brides. Homosexuality was hidden and denied, childhood was innocent. Premarital sexual conduct was regulated in dating rituals. Extramarital sex was furtive. There were rules about what to do, how far to go, who to tell, and the ever-present threat of unwanted pregnancy—the supreme announcement of rebellion, disgrace, wantonness. The female was always perceived as the loser, the one to be pitied. Sex was trouble, female sexuality dangerous. If you were smart, you necked. You kept your desires in tow. You held onto the prize you could give your husband—your "unsullied" body. You married, and felt disappointed if the sexual relationship did not offer all it held out. You wondered why you waited. You felt cheated and frustrated. You made a bargain—you accepted marriage, protection, a home. You taught your daughter to do as you did. And then Kinsey [1] wrote about you and your sexual experiences. He spoke frankly about your real experiences. And you wanted more information and asked for it and then Masters and Johnson [2] responded. Your daughter had access to the pill. She and your son talked of free love and sometimes

---

[1] Alfred C. Kinsey et al., *Sexual Behavior in the Human Female* (Philadelphia: W. B. Saunders, 1953).

[2] William H. Masters and Virginia E. Johnson, *Human Sexual Response* (Boston: Little, Brown, 1966).

practiced it. Sex was out of the closet. Professionals extolled the virtue of it. Older people went for sex counseling, young people experimented, palaces of sexual pleasure opened, sexual swinging became a pastime, women started sleeping with one another openly, and homosexual men moved to New York and San Francisco to create communities.

The dramatic changes in sexual mores in the last fifteen years have not given credence to a post-Freudian and popular notion that underneath the repression of our grandparents and parents lies a free and natural sexuality bursting for expression. Sex and sexuality are, paradoxically, *more* confusing today. We are encouraged to have an active sexual life and we believe it is a good idea. We are exhorted to enjoy sex, physical contact, massage, pleasure, to feel comfortable within our bodies, and to tolerate our children's sexuality. And yet these possibilities we may endorse bring with them a kind of pressure. In reality our sexuality was shaped and formed rather more in line with the values of our grandparents' generation than to suit the staggering array of possibilities on today's sexual market. As these possibilities and our inner thoughts and desires come together, we may feel bewildered and confused, unclear about what we want and what it all means. We may feel that we put too much stress on sex or not enough. We don't know if it is about love, eroticism, passion, connection, tenderness, self-expression, reproduction, dependence, strength, power, and so on. It may be all of those things at different times. Sex has the power to please us more profoundly than we can put into words, or it can alienate and disappoint. Our range of responses depends on our emotional state and that of our partners, on our physical well-being and our personal histories. Each of us has a sexual heritage that is unique. But obviously how we feel and think about our bodies and our sexuality reflect our gender and the sex roles we have absorbed.

*   *   *

Eleanor was a virgin until she married Jim in 1959. This was important to both of them as was the fact that he was "experienced." They didn't question this imbalance, it was just the way things were. Eleanor was "keeping herself" for Jim. Jim wanted his wife to be "pure." What do these two sentences tell us about sexuality in a large percentage of heterosexual couples? Firstly it casts the sexual relationship in terms of ownership and possession. Eleanor delivered her sexuality to her husband. Jim, by marrying her, gave her a place to be sexual. For if she acted on her sexual desires outside of the marriage, or if she were not a virgin, the implication would be that she was "tainted" and "dirty" and *she herself would feel this*. It was believed that when a man married he took responsibility for his wife's sexuality. In a curious way, it was now attached to him, rather than to her. He had rights to it and the responsibility of being experienced. A father had to give his daughter away to his son-in-law intact. Her sexuality passed from one man's protection to another's province. In exchange for bringing her husband her sexuality, Eleanor expected to be economically supported. She in turn would take on the household tasks and the emotional realm of their life together.

Jim had been raised to anticipate regular sex as one of the benefits that went along with being grown up and married. His sexual adventures up to his marriage were goal-oriented. He wanted experience, although what that entailed or meant was never quite spelled out. Eleanor grew up intrigued by her sexuality, this quasi-dangerous, magical "thing" she had to watch out for. She thinks of sexuality in terms of love and commitment. Jim thinks of sexuality in terms of sensation and a good time. Eleanor and Jim are typical of white middle-class people born in the 1930s and 1940s who came of age before the "sexual revolution" of the late 1960s. Their sexual life gradually became less satisfying to them after the first five years of their marriage. They continued to be physically attracted to each other but after the children were born, their sexual contact settled into a routine in which they were sexually intimate about twice a month—an amount judged to be too little by both of them. They were physical with each other in a cozy taken-for-granted way, which both felt was more affectionate than sexual. Their teenage children's sexual explorations put them both through an emotional wringer. They didn't want to stand in the way of the children's adventures. They both believed that their sexuality was somewhat limited by how they had been brought up. They had spent the first years of marriage trying to unravel the restrictions, taboos, and the ordinary ignorance they had both accrued. They saw themselves as broad-minded and liberal and they were hesitant about interfering in their children's affairs, but they were troubled by the kinds of sexual scenes they imagined or knew their kids were involved in. They noticed that their concern with their children coincided with an awareness of how sexually distant from one another they had become. They came for counseling to sort out how to best not interfere with the kids and improve their sexual life together.

What Eleanor and Jim told us about their sexual histories and their sexuality in general has been voiced by many other people in this kind of relationship. When Eleanor and Jim made love for the first time, and by this they meant intercourse, they already knew each other very well. They had been dating for three years, were entwined in each other's lives, and had made plans together about the future. Jim was training to be an electrical engineer and Eleanor decided to become a nutritionist because it would offer flexibility and the possibility of part-time work when she was ready to start raising a family. No draft intervened to separate them and they both went to the local state college. Their families got to know each other quite well, and for a time Jim's cousin dated Eleanor's younger sister. When they married and set up house together they were deeply in love and couldn't wait to show this fully. Although they were both nervous about their first night together, they approached it with tremendous joy, free of guilt or anxiety. Like the vast majority of people of their generation, their sexual relationship was only one current within a much larger relationship that had developed between them. Expressing sexual love with each other without interruption was a logical climax to the emotional terrain they had tilled and nurtured over three years. Their sexual love brought them even closer. They felt connected and committed to each other. During lovemaking they were so utterly engrossed with each other they remembered not knowing whose body was whose; they felt physically fused and totally absorbed by the sensuality they were creating together. Their sexual relationship became a means of communication for them. They interacted less around the daily aspects of life—they didn't fill each other in on the details of what was happening at work and so on—drawing their energy to romantic dinners followed by enraptured lovemaking and conversations in bed in which they couldn't take their eyes or hands off each other. They wondered why anyone did anything else but make love all day. Their sexual relationship brought a deeper state of intimacy, an intimacy that crossed physical boundaries, creating new psychological states in each of them and between them. They became dependent on their sexual relationship to express how they felt about each other. The sex took on particular emotional resonances and tied together in this new way, as they played with each other, seduced each other, exposing their vulnerabilites and the parts of them hidden from the world. They found both security and contentment in this aspect of their marriage. It was a safe, exciting, and mutually satisfying haven they had created together.

The exploits of their children shocked them. They found the contrast between the meaning they had attached to sex and sexuality and the seemingly cavalier attitude their kids affected difficult to reconcile. This discordance within the family led them to reflect on how they saw and experienced their *actual* sexual relationship after eighteen years of married life. They began to face the fact that over the last several years they had become dissatisfied and disappointed with their sexual life together. It didn't feel as expressive, as romantic, as exciting, as meaningful, or as crucial. The sex itself became unimaginative and almost routine. The time before and after sex was not particularly special, the sex neither followed especially good contact, nor opened up the way for it. There was, they both agreed, a comfortable, familiar feel about it. Their sexual communication did not seem to reach them as deeply as in the past. It was reassuring and reasonably enjoyable but did not stand for or signify a particularly meaningful loving exchange.

Later we shall see the dynamics that often unfold in couples bringing them to a point similar to that reached by Eleanor and Jim. But for now let's examine in detail how the underlying psychological themes expressed in the previous chapter can deepen our understanding of the dynamics involved in this kind of sexual situation. When a man and a woman make love in the context of an intimate relationship, they are bonding together and creating something new and bigger than each of them. Their sexual intimacy is more than an appetite, it is a creative act in which each one is giving and being responsive. The desire to make love arises out of the need to express the love in the relationship. The physical and emotional boundaries between two people temporarily dissolve and in their openness and receptivity they create a sexual vocabulary and language. They each bring a different psychology and a different physicality to that creative act and their private sexuality is shaped by the effects of gender in both trivial and fundamental ways.

Eleanor and Jim were both raised according to the notions of femininity and masculinity. We have seen how Eleanor had imposed on her by society a split about female sexuality. She, like all women, couldn't but help be affected by the ideas that those around her held about women and sex. She was brought up to know that her sexuality was highly valued and potentially dangerous and that it needed protecting. Inside, she felt somewhat distanced from these two imperatives and the images of herself as either a virgin princess or a dangerous temptress. She did however feel confined by them and was relieved that she could entrust herself to Jim. When she married she really did not know very much about her body from a sexual point of view. Discouraged from exploring "down there" as a child, learning to be modest about menstrual periods, she entered married life somewhat as a sexual innocent. She had what was considered a "good figure," and this contributed to her feelings of self-esteem. But the theme of alienation was perpetuated by this, for she knew that her figure was an asset that helped her attract and hold her husband. He was very complimentary about her large breasts and Eleanor saw her body and her sexuality as something that she was giving to him. In sexuality as in other aspects of her development Eleanor had learned to be attentive and giving, putting the needs of the other person first and obscuring the vision of her own. She was eager to please Jim and wanted to be a good lover for him. Although she would have described their early sexual life together as mutual, at another level we can see that she was focused on giving Jim pleasure and that her own feelings of contentment and satisfaction depended upon his showing her his pleasure. This dynamic parallels other aspects of being brought up with feminine socialization. Just as Margaret (in chapter I) was meant to gain her satisfactions in life from identifying with her husband's pleasures and accomplishments, so too was Eleanor's sexual pleasure to be funneled through her husband's. Her focus on him was not especially unusual, particularly in the early stage of their marriage. Her sex-role training prepared her to take pleasure in his reflection. Her mother had indicated to her that the sexual side of mar-

riage was not really such a pleasure for a woman and
Eleanor was pleasantly surprised by how much she did
enjoy the sexual aspects of her relationship and how important her sexuality was to her. But her actual experience of sex was typical for her gender. She was dependent on Jim to introduce her to her own body and its
sexual potential. She could not initiate lovemaking—it
would never have occurred to her. She wasn't passive in
bed but a part of her was outside of the experience,
looking on, making sure that Jim was as delighted as he
could be. She would gladly try anything Jim proposed
and felt contented and pleased that she was able to make
him happy. She liked intercourse, although she was not
orgasmic. When Jim entered her she knew that their
lovemaking would finish shortly. She put her whole
body and soul into this part of the lovemaking, holding
him tight, stroking him as she knew he liked. She purred
contentedly when he came and felt satisfied and warm.
His actions framed their lovemaking. She would fix dinner and set a romantic table, she would wear clothes
that she knew Jim found particularly sexy. She made the
sexual environment in which Jim would act and then she
felt good when he made advances toward her, for she
felt that he very much wanted her and needed her in that
way. In their sexual relationship Eleanor was able to feel
that she was very much a wanted person. She felt his
desire for her and this made her feel good. This also
modified the internal experience we have noticed in girls
that is the psychological consequence of being raised as
second-class citizens, the sense that women are not
really valued. Eleanor felt valued and appreciated. Jim
would pursue her, pay her a lot of attention and com-
pliments, and she would feel that she was worthy.

For his part, Jim brought equally stereotypically male
attitudes into his lovemaking with Eleanor. He was very
pleased that he had such a sexy wife. Eleanor was
everything Jim dreamed of and fantasized about. She
was warm, open, receptive, and beautiful. He loved her
soft body and would look forward to being enveloped

by her. She liked to make love often and never refused him. She obviously enjoyed herself and that pleased Jim. He was never nervous approaching her and he never had difficulty having or sustaining an erection. Like many men, Jim couldn't quite put into words the profound contentment that making love gave him. He felt it deeply, but he verbalized it—to his friends, that is—in terms of accomplishment. He took pride in knowing that he could satisfy Eleanor. But could he or did he? Unbeknown to either of them Eleanor and Jim were involved in a complicated series of sexual transactions and communications that took away from their potential pleasure, or to put it another way, their pleasure was cast in a frame that was skewed.

Obviously men and women approach and experience their sexuality and their sexual relationships from very different positions. They have been brought up to relate to their bodies differently. Boys' urinary tracts are external, they come to handle their penises from a very early age. Their sexual organ is a fact of their daily experience. Along with developing an ease with holding their penises to direct the flow of urine, they *see* themselves being able to. This experience of early mastery feeds into the culturally created phenomenon of penis idolization—power and majesty become associated with the male organ. This notion extends to the male body, and boys are encouraged to develop their physical strength and prowess. A young man who is not athletic may feel himself to be unmanly, or perhaps even a weakling. A man is encouraged to use his body as expressive of his power and presence. A woman, by contrast, learns little about her sexual organs and rarely to take pride in them. It is as though they are to be hidden. But at the same time there is great emphasis on a woman being attractive and being able to reflect the current trends in body size and body image. Women tend to be plagued much more than men with confusion about their body image. This is in part because of the strong emphasis on looking the right way, wearing the right clothes, having the right size breasts for this year's image, having the right kind of hair to fit in. It is as though a woman has to put to one side who she is (sexually and physically) and model herself on the images of femininity that adorn the billboards, magazines, newspapers and TV screens. She then puts on this image as best she can and, alienated from her own body, goes in search of a partner, hoping that she has been able to make herself sufficiently attractive to interest a man of her choosing. All women come to feel that their bodies need improving in some way or another. A woman may dislike her nose, or feel her legs are too short. She may feel her thighs are too bulky or her breasts too large or too small. She may feel her tummy sticks out too much or that her muscle tone is shot. In other words, it is hard to meet a woman who doesn't feel that there is some physical aspect of her that she would like to change. The paradox lies in the fact that at the same time as the woman is trying to make herself as pleasing and as sexually attractive to others as possible, she has been discouraged from exploring her own body and sexual organs.

A woman approaches her first sexual relationships then with a certain unease about her body. This may focus on her concern about whether her partner will enjoy her body when she takes off her clothes, but this worry often masks much deeper concerns of whether she will be accepted and whether she will be able to relax sexually. When a woman first goes to bed with a man she is looking for both a good sexual experience as well as hoping that in this relationship she will gain love, attention, and the feeling of being wanted and accepted. Deep inside her, as we have seen, she does not trust that her needs will be met. She hopes that her man will be able to see what she wants and to give it to her, but much of her personality incorporates the unconscious view that she shouldn't expect to have her needs met. Two factors contribute to this expectation. The first is that she herself does not necessarily know what she wants sexually because she has come to have a disjointed relationship with her body. Until very recently, for example, many women did not know about the source of their sexual pleasure. Since Freud and until Masters and Johnson, the clitoris, the female equivalent to the penis, was devalued and dismissed. A lot of hocus-pocus was written in both technical and popular sexual manuals directing husbands to vaginal stimulation in order to ready their wives for penetration. The vulva[3] and the clitoris, if mentioned, were seen as the site of the immature woman's sexual response. The reader was reassured that to give a woman sexual pleasure, a romantic atmosphere and a prolonged period of foreplay followed by intercourse would do the trick. Implicit in these instructions was the idea that female sexuality was indeed different, for women needed an emotional atmosphere and a prolonged, that is, overly long, stimulation (as though what men needed was the norm). Women reading these books couldn't help but pick up the message that a man was doing her a favor, that his sexual needs were more straightforward and compact, that there was something special, even a bit awkward and cumbersome about female sexuality. In this, as in other aspects of women's needs, women may have come to feel that their desires and wants are a bit too much. They may feel guilty and awkward if, for example, oral sex pleases them and brings them to orgasm. They may fear that it is taking altogether too long for them to reach orgasm and that their man will lose interest or be bored. They may be so concerned with their partner's thoughts and feelings and so disbelieving that they are truly interested and eager to give that they cannot take in and enjoy what is being given. *Therefore, they may be hurrying to relieve their partners of the burden of having to give to them.* Women try to escape from this because unaccustomed as they are to

---

[3] Dr. Harriet Lerner has importantly called attention to the use of the term *vulva* to describe women's entire genital area.

getting, when they *do* receive this kind of love and attention it touches off their desires for it, their shame about wanting, and their disbelief that someone is giving to them.

The second factor influencing a woman's negative expectations of sexual fulfillment is the fact that she is likely to be far too preoccupied with giving to her partner sexually to be concerned about her own needs. She had read that the most legitimate expression of heterosexual love is intercourse and simultaneous orgasm. And so she endeavors to make this happen. Because she so wants her partner to be happy, and indeed feels her own happiness through this, she applies the same kind of attentiveness to lovemaking that she does in intuiting his emotional needs. She conveys to him that he should let her know what he wants, creating an environment in which his needs are welcomed.

A woman then is afflicted in the following ways when she enters her first heterosexual relationships. She is distanced from her body, often ignorant about its sexual potential, preoccupied with her partner's experience, and unused to receiving.

When a man starts up a sexual relationship he may also be somewhat uneasy. He too is distanced from his sexuality. He approaches sex as though it were a challenge. Giving a woman sexual satisfaction becomes the goal. But the accomplishment is propelled less by altruistic motives and more by needs that actually prevent him from getting to know a woman's sexuality. There is no such thing as one view of female sexuality. For him, female sexuality is a conglomerate of the myriad of images displayed before him daily. Women's sexuality seems to be all around him and yet untouchable. Women's bodies sell him everything from soap to cars. Women are seducers as well as the prize. He has to juggle pictures of movie star goddesses, the women in his everyday life, and his fantasies when choosing a lover. His sexuality is seen as more physical than emotional, although sexual encounters for him fill very important needs.

A man very much wants to please a woman sexually. But as we have seen, men looking to learn from sex manuals or from other men by and large find information that is inadequate, for it reflects *men's* ideas about women's sexuality rather than detailing women's actual experience of sex.

Joe, a writer now in his thirties and living happily with Monika, recalls, "When I was in my late teens and twenties the whole sex business was really touch and go for me. I knew the most important thing was to make a girl come and I was always worried that I wouldn't be able to keep going long enough to satisfy her. My basic knowledge was simply this. You spent a lot of time juicing a woman up—just till you thought she was about to come. Mainly you did this by making sure she was wet and touching around the general vaginal area—hoping you were doing it right—and then, when I thought she was ready, I would enter her and hope that I wouldn't come right away. In one way I was very involved with giving her pleasure, but in another way I see now that I didn't have a clue about what I was doing. I felt really good if I thought she was satisfied and—here's the crazy part—not because it made her especially happy, at least it didn't seem to, but because I felt manly. I suppose now I see it is a bit self-involved and like a test. If she came, my self-esteem rose. It wasn't too much about showing love, it was more about achieving some difficult feat." He went on: "It wasn't until Monika and I got together that I got a whole new perspective on it and had to face that probably all that macho business didn't add up to much. One of the main things I think now is that I was so concerned about doing it right I never stopped to ask or to find out if it was really nice for *her*."

Joe was a victim, like so many men, to misinformation and a macho self-image. He was caught up on proving his sexual prowess to himself to an extent that prevented him from being much more than a technician rather than the lover he wanted to be. He hid his vulnerability and his anxieties behind an image of surety and virility. In fact, he wasn't even aware of the fact that he was tense or insecure because his sexually eager and capable image worked fairly successfully for him.

So we can see how the same dynamics of the unequal exchange between women's and men's needs play out in the sexual arena. A woman is preoccupied with a man's needs because that is where she has learned to spend her attention. Her discomfort with her own sexual needs and her body and her disbelief that anyone will give to her or be there for her prevent her from articulating her desires. The man meanwhile is unaware of how ignorant he really is about female sexuality. He assumes he knows what is going on and what a woman wants because his upbringing and experience with women have fostered the belief that whatever he knows is correct. His vulnerabilities are locked behind layers and layers of socialization so that he can't easily bring them out into the open, examine them, and engage with them. Both sexes are working on fragile premises, the woman always thinking others know best, which, of course isn't true, the man thinking he knows best, which is equally untrue.

Rosemary and Neil's relationship shows another facet of what sexuality is meant to convey. Although they had been living together for ten years, Rosemary was terribly insecure. Neil could never tell her that he loved her and Rosemary lived with the constant worry that he would leave her for someone else. She stayed with him because she loved him (see chapter III), always hoped things would change, and that he would be more open—as indeed he was when he relaxed by having a few drinks or smoking pot. Rosemary was sexually inexperienced when she met Neil. He was her first lover and she was very happy to get together with him. Although Neil had not had that many girlfriends he projected an aura of confidence and experience in sexual matters—especially as compared to Rosemary. Rosemary saw Neil as much more knowledgeable about sex than

she and relied on him to take the initiative both as to
when they would make love and how they made love. As
the relationship continued their lovemaking gradually
became more and more infrequent. Rosemary made
attempts to get things going sexually but Neil did not
respond to her advances and was a bit disdainful.
Rosemary in turn felt hurt and rejected and eventually
was loath to come on to Neil, even though she wanted to
make love. She waited instead for his infrequent urges.

The actual quality of their lovemaking was not that
splendid but Rosemary longed for the physical contact,
the hugging, stroking, and holding that were part of
it. Beyond that, though, the sexual encounters had symbolic significance. Rosemary desperately wanted acceptance and reassurance that Neil loved her, and this
longing was transferred into craving symbols of acceptance such as having regular sex. It was not so important
to her what transpired in the sexual encounter; what was
important was that it showed her she was wanted. Neil
would get incensed with her if she asked him to show his
commitment directly, shouting, ''Isn't living with you
proof enough that I care!'' He made Rosemary feel that
she was wanting too much. And because Rosemary was
always showing how much she wanted and needed him,
he never had to confront his own needs for her. We can
see the cha-cha dynamic in their sexual relationship. The
more she wanted, the more he backed off. When she
was able to be caught up in her work and not so appar-
ently interested in or in need of him, Neil would approach her sexually.

In actual fact, Neil was afraid and uncomfortable
with his own sexuality and he was somewhat scared of
Rosemary's. Before Rosemary he had gone out with a
few women but had never formed a close attachment.
He was scared of women and of women's sexuality. It
seemed very mysterious and powerful. He realized he
was scared of making love and particularly frightened
of intercourse, because during intercourse he had experienced the most elemental feelings of being connected

to Rosemary and he found these feelings extremely disconcerting.

During lovemaking, the physical boundaries that separate one human being from another dissolve. The sensations that can be aroused are powerful and stir up feelings that are hard to put into words. For Neil, intercourse itself was always wonderful. He described it as giving him a sense of being totally at ease and exhilarated at the same time. He felt good, warm, and content. He felt accepted and whole at a very deep level. It was like losing consciousness and at the same time being terribly alive. He felt merged with Rosemary as though they were one. After lovemaking, however, he would feel incredibly depressed and let down. He didn't know why, because moments before he had felt so very close. He would want to go off by himself or turn over and go to sleep, to separate himself from Rosemary, to shake her out of him.

As we examined Neil's desire for and avoidance of sex between the two of them, it turned out that he was terrified by having such strong feelings with a woman. It made him feel vulnerable, helpless, as though he was losing power and control. He couldn't bear to be in a woman's power—as he saw it—even though the sexual experience was so ecstatic for him. It scared him to feel so close to someone that he was merged. In therapy he came to realize that avoiding intercourse was just one way in which his fear of being close to Rosemary showed itself. He realized that he often did not satisfy Rosemary sexually but kept her dangling. As long as she was vaguely unsatisfied, Rosemary was clingy, always wanting some form of contact with Neil. Although Neil felt rejecting of that part of Rosemary, it allowed him to see her as the dependent one in the relationship.

Rosemary pointed out that whenever she did feel sexually satisfied she was aware of a different quality in her attachment to Neil. She felt as though she wasn't looking to him for reassurance all the time but was feeling contented and at peace with herself. She didn't feel she was desperately seeking connection or contact. When he was rejecting or distant, and she couldn't rely on their sexual encounters to get close, she felt cast out and anxious. She pursued him but projected a worry that she would be turned away.

The fear of merger that Neil expressed is felt by women, too. For in lovemaking, especially where two people feel very close, the physical and emotional pleasure that two people can create together often touches off echoes of our very earliest experiences in the world when we were merged with mother. In this original merger we were indeed somewhat helpless, we did not yet have language to make our needs known. We relied on mother's sensitivity to create an accepting environment. Our world was essentially sensual. In it we experienced bliss and discomfort. We could not control these feelings. We could only hope that mother knew when we were hungry or could tell when our diapers were cold and wet. We were suspended in a physical world without the physical strength to make things happen for us. And beyond the vulnerability that our physical smallness and immaturity aroused, the echo of the merger with mother reevokes our struggle in trying to differentiate from her, to be different, to separate ourselves psychologically, to need her less.

In sex, we are plunged once again into a world awash with physical sensual expression. We lose the studied and conscious sense of ourselves. Our physical and emotional armor temporarily dissolves and we melt into an experience of oneness. We find the mate we've longed for. We are each reunited with the warming, accepting aspects of mother. We long to be engulfed, surrounded, and enclosed in a physical emotional orbit. In heterosexual love, men make a symbolic reentry into that mysterious, soft, all-embracing world. For a woman the (usually) larger body of the man holding her symbolizes that original merger. These resonances with the infant state before separation-individuation arouse in all of us complicated reactions, as we have seen in chapter III.

At the same time that we can give ourselves up to the embrace of that psychophysical state, we wish to escape it. For when we feel so close to another person that the physical boundaries between us have been crossed, we may feel the precariousness of our psychological boundaries. We play out an adult version of the struggle to separate from mother. We may be scared by our loved one's ability to get under our skin. We may be shocked to discover how we find ourselves in our partner's love. We may run from the recognition of our urgency to connect. We may try to shake off the depth of our adult connection by denying our dependency and need for each other. We both yearn for and are wary of the quality of that early infantile dependency.

The dissolving of the psychophysical boundaries that occurs in heterosexual love can be even more pronounced in a lesbian relationship. Gillian and Rose both had been sexually involved with men before they became lovers. In fact, when they first started sleeping together, Rose was still living with and having occasional sex with her husband. Both of them were enthralled by their love affair and by the ways in which they approached sex together. It was so different than their heterosexual experiences. They both felt shy and vulnerable but at the same time relaxed and responsive. Neither felt they had to show each other the way or be the one in control. They could learn together what pleased them and they felt free of an internal pressure to hurry up. They were comfortable exploring the delights of each other's bodies, at once so similar and so different. They both felt more involved and swept up in this relationship than ever before and were able, because of loving each other's bodies, to allow that acceptance of femininity to reflect in themselves. They both noticed a new appreciation of their own bodies, which accompanied a drop in the level of their preoccupation with the "faults" of their respective physical appearances. They were enormously happy sexually. They didn't hesitate to find out what pleased each other, and they were both good givers. The only perplexing aspect of their sexual relationship was what followed immediately after sex. It was as though they went through a process in which they had to physically disengage. One of them, usually Rose, would jump out of bed, and spend ages in the shower. At first Gillian was very hurt by this but then she appreciated being on her own for a bit. They both noticed this physical distancing and neither of them exactly knew what was going on. Rose thought that perhaps she felt guilty that the lovemaking was so good and that like many people having clandestine affairs she was trying to wash Gillian out of her system. But this explanation didn't make nearly as much sense to her as the visual picture she had of their entwinement and the absolute contentment it aroused in her. What they both realized was that they had been so merged during the lovemaking and so very taken up in it and by it that they really didn't feel a sense of their own physical boundaries. Having a brief separation right after lovemaking pulled them back into themselves. Their merger touched off fears in both of them that they would be stuck together, lose their own identity and be consumed by the other.

As we have seen, the process of girls separating from mother is a difficult one. Mother, because of her shared gender identity, relates to her daughter as though she were an extension of herself. This makes it hard for the daughter to know herself apart from mother. On top of this, mother often has not been able to give steady nurturing to her daughter because of the push-pull dynamic. As we saw with Katie in chapter I, and with so many of the women we have met on these pages, the daughter then moves away from mother with trepidation, not terribly sure in her own boundaries, feeling somewhat insecure and shaky about her sense of self as different from her mother. When two women open themselves up to each other in a close sexual relationship, they may both be touched by echoes of that early merger with mother. They may both long to be reunited now, in this adult way, with a warm, soft, loving, accepting woman. They may be overwhelmed by how much pleasure they experience and by how easily their boundaries dissolve and they feel the possibility of merger.

When boys are separating from mother, they and mother use the fact of their gender difference in that process. Boys rely on these differences in the creating of boundaries that then help them differentiate psychologically.[4] The development of a masculine psychology has at its roots the need to differentiate and separate from a woman. This poses psychological problems for men when they get close to a woman. They unconsciously fear a loss not just of a separate identity but of their masculine identity. They may perceive the echoes in the merger in intercourse as a regression and fear reincorporation with mother. This unconscious fantasy prevents many men from getting as close to and sustaining the intimacy that is in their heterosexual relationship.

The fear of the loss of masculinity from the merger is but one side of a precarious sense of masculinity wrought by our gendered system. The overvaluation of the penis, the visible manifestation that one is indeed different from mother, arises in part out of this need to demythologize mother, and hence all women, in our psychic worlds. A male organ is utilized for real boundaries and is then invested with the power to "do" things to women. A man's penis becomes for him a symbol of his power and control over women, but it has another, more hidden, function: It is for him a crucial reassurance of his separateness and difference from, first, his mother, and, later, from all women. The sense of masculinity rests on a notion, perhaps a buried one, of males as the other, different, not like females. It is

---

[4] They may live much more rigidly behind these boundaries on a day-to-day basis and approach situations and relationships with what appears to be a clear sense of self, even if the origins of this sense of self are arrived at somewhat precariously: that is, in opposition or defensively.

ironic that this very sense of other has found a cultural translation in patriarchy in the exclusion of women from political, economic, social, sexual, and legal equity, so that it is the woman who becomes the outsider and carries the emotional burden of being the other. A man's believing the penis to be the center of his being and an instrument of control and power over women illustrates another way in which men's fear of facing their dependency needs adds to difficulties in the bedroom.

Men and women are fearful of female sexuality. The very idea of it is so threatening that until very recently a woman in her twenties to forties who was not attached to a man was desexualized as a spinster or oversexualized as a nymphomaniac. A middle-aged woman interested in sex was the subject of embarrassment, a young divorcée or widow seemed to ignite sexual fears and fantasies in a well-established social group. Female sexuality was believed to be mysterious, unknowable, that it must be contained. Here's Johnny, a thirty-six-year-old teacher, reflecting on the impact of his upbringing: "I think men grow up to feel that we are always supposed to be ready for sex and that women are really reluctant. The sexpots in the movies contradicted the idea, but they only existed on celluloid, which was a relief, because God knows what I would have done with a real Ava Gardner. I was supposed to be able to turn a woman on, drive her out of her mind, and all the time stay on top of the situation myself. Once I was involved with a woman, Anne, who was totally wild sexually. She just gave herself up to the situation. It was great but pretty hairy there for a while because I was worried that I couldn't meet her excitement. I would feel a bit left out and overwhelmed and out of control. I think I feel easier when a woman matches my excitement. If she surpasses it in a way that I notice, I feel like there's a demand on me I might not know how to meet."

Johnny talked about the two ways that not being in control affected him. He felt potentially inadequate and that he could lose the self-esteem he derived from "satisfying a woman." If a woman was very into herself sexually, and he wasn't responsible for introducing her to her sexual potential, managing her sexuality by pushing the right buttons and controlling what happened when he did, then he felt the woman would not need him and would be separate. "For me it's a question of her not being in the sex for me but for herself," he explained. "This makes me angry, I feel neglected. I can feel that she's abandoned me. It's one thing if I give her an orgasm and she's being nice to me by accepting it. It's another if she's in there for herself."

When Johnny was involved with Anne, the siren, he was scared about losing her all the time. When she left the apartment in the morning looking smashing, he would feel annoyed that she was showing the world her sexuality. Her display made him feel insecure and uneasy. He couldn't stand it and they broke off when in a fight he called her a "whore."

Johnny drifted from this relationship into a series of one-night stands and casual encounters. In these liaisons he was searching for instant contact without much involvement. His self-esteem was at a low point and he sought out women in singles bars hoping to be taken home by one of them. But the women he was attracted to there all seemed to be eager to be in a relationship rather than want the casual sex he was looking for. He found himself sleeping with several different women, feeling close during the sex, but with little desire to pursue a relationship. He wasn't really ready to get involved with anyone and he sought the sexual encounters as a substitute to relating. The women would listen to his problems, try to soothe away his upset and offer him a warm and sensual body to lie with through the night. He was able to get the benefits of women's nurturing skills at a point when he was feeling vulnerable and shaky without making a commitment he wasn't ready for.

Sheila, a twenty-eight-year-old assistant record pro-

ducer who hung out in singles bars, was clear that she
was only looking for one-night stands too. In these encounters she sought confirmation that she was attractive
and could interest a man. She did not expect tenderness
or an especially receptive ear; she relied on her female
friends for these things. She was proving to herself that
she was appealing. At the bar she was quite forward in
going after the men she wanted. She enjoyed being able
to choose and to be active rather than wait for the men
to pick her out. About twice a week she took a new man
home with her, although she didn't let anyone spend the
whole night. Internally she was involved in a struggle
between two different parts of herself. One part of her
desperately wanted to be involved in an ongoing sexual
relationship and another part of her didn't. Of course
the situation was not as straightforward as that. Sheila
despaired of ever meeting anyone she would really like
and trust. She had been badly hurt by Fred when he
unexpectedly left her for a man. Fred had been very
emotionally present and warm. Not dazzling sexually
but certainly attentive, and she had felt very close to
him. Although she later learned that he had always been
more attracted to men and his decision to break up with
her and become involved with Bob had been an agon-
izing one for him, she couldn't help translate his homosexuality as a rejection of her. In her twice-weekly bar
ritual she was constantly involved in testing out her attractiveness, and once having reassured herself that she
could indeed attract the men that appealed to her, she
would lose interest in them. Each encounter expressed
both the love she wanted and at the same time reaf-
firmed its impossibility.

Sheila and Johnny both used sex in the singles scene
in order to be in the rejecting role. They both derived
boosts to their self-esteem in the process. Johnny would
find attentive, solicitous women. Sheila got constant
confirmation of her sex appeal and attractiveness. She
was trying to undo the rejection of her femininity that
she experienced with Fred. For both of them, one-night

stands were a way to have warmth and contact within safely proscribed boundaries in which their dependency needs did not leak out more than either of them could handle. On the surface they both felt good that they didn't need to be in a relationship.

The search for a partner in life, someone with whom to share and create a personal world, is shaped by a complex of factors. For many couples the sexual aspect of the relationship is a dynamic force from the beginning, even if, like Eleanor and Jim, the sex was not consummated for several years. Sexual attraction between two people is an important binder and curiously this is so whether or not the sex is satisfactory. In choosing a partner, we are first drawn to the physical presence of another. How they hold themselves, what they project about themselves, what they are wearing, how they move in their bodies and so on. We may be physically attracted to someone who, when we get to know her or him, does not fulfill our expectations and so the sexual attraction evaporates. We may generate fantasies about strangers because we feel erotically responsive. Our capacity to be responsive connects with a desire to relate, to get physically close. Even in a one-night stand we seek an intense connection. The desire for physical expression and release occurs in a relationship, however transitory.

What we see in another is often a reflection of how we see ourselves. We choose partners who mirror and complement our own self-image or have attributes we long for. Jane loved Saul's gracefulness, height and leanness. She was little and cute, a bundle of energy. She seemed receptive. They both dressed fairly modishly and complemented each other. When they first met, Jane remembers thinking, "I hope he is as interesting as he is good looking." She went for his physical type but was often disappointed at parties when a man's personality did not match his good looks.

Our sexual desire can be stimulated by the shape of a

hand, the wiggle of a hip, the look in someone's eyes. Any part of the body can become an area that another finds erotic. When we are sexually attracted to someone, conjuring up a picture of how she or he looks can spark off gentle sexual feelings. Many people feel this way about their partners ten, fifteen, or twenty years after living with and being sexual with them. Deidre was married to David for eighteen years. She would look at him sitting and reading across the room, and feel warm and tender toward him. These feelings did not carry over to the bedroom, however. They made love regularly and it was physically enjoyable, but she could hardly remember the last time she felt passionate or full of desire. She missed the urgency of their early lovemaking and wondered how something once so pressing had become routine and pedestrian. We have heard this complaint so often that we are bound to ask what happens to the sexual ardor in a long-term relationship. Why does the passion in so many relationships get tamed? Why is there so frequently a downward spiral of interest and deep enjoyment? How does being emotionally dependent and more or less secure affect the texture of our sexual relationships? Of course not all sexual relationships provide less satisfaction or deteriorate over time, but many do, and many people have the experience of being sexually dulled, of going to bed night after night knowing that sex is not on the agenda.

Some of the reasons are fairly obvious. As you spend more time with each other and are involved in the process of sharing a life together, sexuality does not become the exclusive area for the expression of close personal intimacy. Living together involves, to one extent or another, cooking together, chatting, sitting cozily by the fire, taking walks, doing domestic chores. These activities all become vehicles for sharing and take on their own particular meaning in the life of a couple. For Saul and Jane, cooking together was not only a sensual pleasure, it was a creative expression of their involvement with each other. They worked together in the kitchen almost wordlessly, Saul stirring Jane's pot, Jane adding seasoning to a dish Saul started. They communicated so much without speaking and they trusted each other completely, enjoying the innovations and building on the repertoire each brought to the marriage. They harmonized beautifully in the kitchen and never once had a row. They enjoyed the whole cooking process from preparation to eating together; it was a shared intimate experience. The energy originally riveted on the sexual aspect of their relating was now somewhat diverted into cooking and other activities. They both wondered why their sex wasn't so passionate but they weren't aware of being dissatisfied with each other.

When a couple falls in love, the reality of the outside world is temporarily pushed back by the intensity of the emotional nesting going on. But soon, and only slowly at first, the couple has to come to grips with their relationship as a part of the world. As the couple "hatches," the magically intense membrane within which they lived dissolves. Each member of the couple introduces the other into her and his world. The integration of the other into one's life has the effect of narrowing the distance between private life and the public world. As these worlds become more aspects of each other there is an impact on the sexual communications. This, the most private of communications, may change ever so slightly. It is no longer as special, as separate, as preserved or as protected. Like eating together, it takes on a variety of meanings. Sometimes it is romantic and extraordinary, often it is approached unthinkingly out of habit, sometimes it is a desire on the part of one member of the couple that the other is happy to respond to but isn't inspired by. The ordinary weariness of life seeps into all of our activities. Sex and love stay protected in the bubble for only a relatively short time.

Living together for several years can create a state of "taking the other for granted." This state can occur with positive or negative results. In most couples this has a mixed effect. On the positive side, taking one's partner for granted may occur because one is able to rely on her or his being there. Secure in the relationship, the person is not constantly caught up in worrying about being left and deserted. But one may also "take a partner for granted" because one has stopped really relating directly. The couple may have become so enmeshed in the transference aspects of the relationship that they are not really aware of who the other person actually is and what her or his needs are. For example, if each partner is carrying a mother transference toward the other, they may imagine both that the other is not really there for them and yet will never really leave. This negative "taking for granted" phenomenon has its toll in the sexual aspects of a relationship. Because one may be unaware of the other person's needs in the relationship a real distance grows that the sexual encounter cannot necessarily bridge in a truly satisfying way. The sex is based on each person's ideal of who the other is rather than on a shared knowledge and intimacy. Hoping that sex can overcome the distance and the distortions inevitably leads to disappointment, and unsatisfying sex does not build an appetite for more. The sexual encounter becomes a means to make contact—one that fails.

When a relationship moves into a phase in which each partner takes the other for granted, the relationship is essentially a frozen one. The transactions and communications are hedged in by fear and innuendo. Each partner "knows" what upsets the other and often stays away from discussing it, scared to tip the equilibrium that has been established. Certain topics may become taboo, or at least difficult to explore, and so a rigidity develops. Not only is each partner not really seen, each can begin to conform to the picture the other holds, by not bringing certain aspects of the self into the relationship. This dynamic not only affects the sexual relationship, it also occurs within it. Many couples with whom we have talked and counseled have a fear of exposing their sexual needs, which then translates into an unwillingness to find out each other's. For example, we found out in couple counseling with Eleanor and Jim, the couple who had married in the late fifties when the sexual mores and knowledge about female sexual response were different than today, that about four years into their sexual relationship, as Eleanor came to know her body better, her sexual desires changed and she very much wanted to be stimulated orally. Once when she and Jim had oral sex she experienced her first orgasm. She was somewhat ashamed of this because she felt that it should have occurred during intercourse. After this first orgasm, she began to masturbate on her own but she felt very guilty about it. She felt that Jim should be giving her that kind of pleasure, rather than herself, and that ideally she should be able to come when he had his orgasm during intercourse. As she was able to satisfy herself, she became less fully present in their sex together and very confused about the situation. Jim felt something had changed slightly but didn't know what and didn't want to pressure her. They got into a routine of making love a couple of times a week, but looking back on it she realized the sex between them was a disappointment. For Jim's part, her withdrawal made him feel less relaxed and open sexually. They settled into a formula of lovemaking except for special occasions. As the sex became more routine it became less and less passionate for both of them. They took each other's moves for granted, could predict the course of feelings that would transpire for both of them. Eleanor meanwhile felt guilty and Jim started to develop active fantasies of what he would like to have going on in bed. Eleanor had internalized the prejudiced ideas about intercourse being "the real thing" and could not bring herself to tell Jim what she wanted. He didn't know what was going on with her and he was unable to ask her if she needed something to change in the lovemaking. He was also scared to show her that something was missing for him. He felt a bit ashamed of his fantasies and didn't know how to tell her about them. The passion got tamed then, because neither of them could really talk about this

nonverbal activity easily. They settled for a minimum of
sexual connection because they weren't able to look at
what was going on between them for many years.

Couple counseling facilitated Eleanor and Jim talking
about their sexual relationship. Eleanor was able to tell
Jim what she enjoyed and he was relieved to have this
information and to know what had been going on. Jim
now felt delighted to integrate Eleanor's pleasures into
their lovemaking. The spoken communications opened
up their sexual relationship and they approached it
again with vigor and excitement.

Talking about the change in regularity of sexual relations, in the quality of those relations, and in the interest in them seems to be an extremely charged issue for
many people in a long-term relationship. This in itself
already tells us something, for the very fact that people
are uncomfortable about looking at their sex lives in-
dicates a certain unease, a disappointment, a shame that
things aren't as they should be.

Often one partner in a couple has a misperception
about the other's level of satisfaction or dissatisfaction.
There may be a sexual cha-cha going on that isn't even
acknowledged, for the individuals perceive their needs
differently. But the fact that a couple so finely tuned at
an emotional level to the ups and downs of the relationship and to the moods of each other can be so oblivious
to each other's sexual dissatisfaction is extremely revealing. Women and men come to sex with different expectations and different needs. For example, men look to
sex to affirm their identity. In lovemaking they assert
their masculinity and it is powerfully reflected back to
them. It bolsters their male identity, which is less stable
than might at first appear. Women often trade sex as
though it were a commodity in their search for security,
warmth, affection, love, and economic protection.
Women approach sex looking for connection. Men
come to it for contact too but also to confirm their difference apart from women. These unconscious threads
that propel our sexual encounters mean that often men

and women are not meeting in the bedroom but are looking for very different things, which neither of them knows about. A partner's perception that he or she isn't having enough sex and the other partner's sense that she or he is then illustrates these different needs.

So far we have been able to elucidate some of the dynamics of sexual relationships from the perspective of how sex-role education prepares and does not prepare us for the bedroom. As we have seen, in all intimate relationships there is both the current person that each partner is relating to and the transference overlays that affect our perceptions of our partners, our hopes of who they can be for us, our projections, and our disappointments.

If we remember the psychological picture we have drawn of women and men, we recall that at each developmental stage, beginning with the texture of that first early dependency on the caretaking mother, girls and boys are related to based on their gender. Their passage from that early dependency to separation-individuation structures their psyches in gender-linked ways. Girls' shared gender with mother and the social meaning of that similarity in patriarchy create the push-pull dynamic in the mother-daughter relationship. This means that girls often don't receive enough nurturance to separate from a position of wholeness. The attempt to separate and become one's own person is extremely difficult. And consequently, girls grow up feeling needy, perplexed as to why they are related to inconsistently. They internalize the rejection, feel ashamed of the desire to be cared for emotionally, and are in an unconscious search for a mother who will relate differently and love them better. Women bring these longings to their sexual relationships, whether these are with men or with women.

Boys' separation from mother is also difficult. Mothers have complex conscious and unconscious feelings about raising sons in a patriarchy, and this is reflected in the ways of relating between a mother and son. At one moment the son may be the recipient of mother's (and father's) idealization of the little prince, and at another he may suffer the effects of mother's unconscious rage, envy, and contempt for the meaning of being male in our society. When boys try to separate from mother, they may also not have received sufficient nurturing—although the expectation of getting stays with them. More importantly for its implications in terms of male-female sexual relationships, the boy, in distinguishing himself, is involved in a process of separating from the feminine aspects of self that he has internalized and attempting to distance himself from mother whose emotional world has held him. He is helped to suppress these aspects of self in the passage through boyhood to manhood, and these important parts of who he is are compartmentalized, sometimes so deeply hidden that the man knows nothing about them, or they may emerge in extremely upsetting ways as was the case with Neil. For most men, though, this part of them is encouraged to come out the most in the intimacy of their sexual relationships. Particularly in heterosexual relationships, women work hard to create an atmosphere in which the man will feel comfortable enough to bare his soul, show his insides, expose his vulnerabilities and the tender side of his personality.

Just as women are involved in an unconscious search for a mother in life who will love them unconditionally, so too do men want the kind of attentiveness, nurturance, and caring that we associate with mothering. In heterosexual love, both partners may experience a temporary loss of psychophysical boundaries and in the merger a dual transference may be in process in which each partner is also reunited with the longed-for mother. This aspect of a sexual relationship can, as we saw with Neil and Rosemary or Gillian and Rose, be experienced as frightening, for it exposes the longing to experience as an adult the holding embrace of a safe womb. However, not all the transferential aspects of this merger are problematic. The experience of being temporarily merged and satisfied in that merger can contribute to a person's sense of well-being. In love and in sex, there are many unconscious factors that lie beneath the surface that motivate us in ways, which, if examined, would seem to have little to do with "healthy," loving impulses. But in love and in lovemaking, there is a process of repair to the low self-esteem and sense of self that so many people suffer. For *being loved* allows us to see and experience ourselves differently. We are taking in the love that another is giving (even if he or she may be giving in part out of narcissistic needs). This love can enter into the well of longing or the emptiness that lives deep inside of us. It can feed us in profoundly important ways and transform deeply held images of unconnectedness. The change that it can produce at an internal level may then change the shape of what each partner is wanting and needing in the sexual relationship. For if as a result of the merger we are able to internalize the loving connection with our partner, that very connection may become dialectically transformed. Sexual closeness may be able to divest itself of the driven aspects of narcissistic relating. Being loved may help two people experience a sense of self-sufficiency strong enough to permit them to begin to relate out of a new wholeness rather than out of a desperate need to fill the void. The connection is now rephrased. This phenomenon occurred in Eleanor and Jim's relationship. Of course there were other factors that contributed to their sexuality being less intense on a regular basis, but part of the shift had to do with this phenomenon of being loved making them feel very different about themselves, very much surer of themselves, and, hence, not so driven to find a meaning or a context totally in each other's life. Their sex became less frenzied then, because its early intensity had contained elements related to issues of transference and narcissistic needs. When these needs were met, the sex no longer became the vehicle to carry them.

*   *   *

At surface range the theme of dependency may not be visible, especially the man's, but as we look at the sexual relationship, trying to understand how men's and women's needs for contact, nurturance, and dependency intersect, a complicated picture unfolds, which reveals at the same moment the paradox of men's expectation of getting coupled with their unease at exposing their vulnerability and their needs. Women meanwhile often substitute sex and sexuality for the emotional contact they so desperately want and don't find sufficiently in their heterosexual relationships. For both, sex serves as a highly charged symbolic expression of generally inarticulated dependency needs.

V

❖ ❖ ❖

The Effect of Pregnancy on the Dependency Dynamic

The decision to have a child is a milestone in the life of a couple. When two people want to have a child together they are making a statement about their feelings for each other. A child represents merger and intimacy in the couple relationship. Just as the two people have created a relationship and nourished loving feelings between them they create a new life. Achieving love and intimacy has a sense of forward movement, a working toward and creating a future together. Reproducing a child together also represents this move forward and the belief in life and growth. The birth of a child represents both the merger of two people as well as the transforming quality of love—that is, just as an intimate relationship allows and demands that a person change and grow so too does a baby represent transformation, growth, newness, development.

Pregnancy sparks off specific issues around the theme of dependency for the expectant couple. For there is the anticipated dependency of the baby and the realization that infants are vulnerable and need care, attention, and love. Mothers and fathers relate to this challenge in gender-linked ways. A mother may worry about whether she can give sufficiently, while a father may be preoccupied with thoughts about whether he can be a good provider. Although the biological imperatives for creating a baby require mutual and equal participation of the two partners, child-rearing arrangements in our society are such that the equality is immediately unbalanced upon the birth of the child. Women raising children have a different relationship to their children than men do. There is an imbalance in the contact, the understanding, the intimacy between mother and child and father and child. The couple who view the nurturing of a child as a mutual experience, a shared experience, are knocked off course, unbeknown to them, because of the child-rearing arrangements that have women as the primary caretakers and men somewhere in the background or off to the side. Women spend the majority of time with the infant, they are responsible for learning to understand the meanings of various cries, they are the ones upon whom the infant depends for her or his very survival. The dependency of an infant is so great that it often creates a shift in the dependency dynamic that existed for the couple before the birth of the child.

For many women, the fact of being pregnant brings with it feelings of self-esteem, accomplishment, confidence, and self-respect. A woman may change so that she no longer seeks a certain confirmation from her partner. Her self-image shifts. She finds a good sense of herself through her pregnancy. Many women report feeling more dependent on their partners during pregnancy. They feel a bit more vulnerable and begin to feel the burden of responsibility for this new life inside them. With this major, new responsibility they become more aware of their own need for someone to rely on and trust. Some men find this time rewarding, because caring for the woman allows them to feel more a part of the birth process. They enjoy feeling needed in this way. It may be one of the few times when men can experience their own desires and abilities to nurture. The caring a man feels for his woman is a direct caring for the baby to come. He cannot feel the life inside of his own body and he needs the woman to share her body, to let him be a part of the physical nurturance during pregnancy. Some men have difficulties with a woman's increased dependency during pregnancy. They may unconsciously feel frightened of her need; they may feel inadequate to the situation, which they imagine to be awesome; they may feel controlled or trapped by her increased dependency and the impending dependency of the coming child. With the birth of the child there now is the chance for the man to care directly for the child. He now has direct access and no longer has the frustration of feeling outside of the situation.

The existence of a third person, a visibly dependent person, in what was previously a household of two, is a dramatic change. The birth of a child not only alters the emotional environment in which the couple lives, but the child also brings new dimensions to the lives of each parent. Each parent must respond in her and his own ways to the child's dependency needs. Dependency as a theme is squarely on the agenda. This is a time when the couple can renegotiate their own dependency with each other as they develop a relationship to their new child, who is utterly dependent on them. In the last chapter we addressed the significance of this shared parenting and its impact on dependency and emotional and psychological life. Because, for the most past, we were all raised by our mothers (especially in the first year of life) and because, by and large, this is still the practice in most families today, we describe here the effects of dependency in a family where mother raises the children.

Because of the dissimilarity in women's and men's emotional dependency needs and because women are the caretakers of infants and children we can see a serious flaw in our society's system for raising children. That is because women as mothers usually feel emotionally deprived themselves, and because they feel so hungry for emotional nurturance they look to their children to fill this emptiness. This "unhealthy" dynamic is built into the structure of our society. After all, from the time she was a little girl herself the woman was taught to feel that her fulfillment in life would come when she was a mother. Society believes the highlight of every woman's life comes with marriage and then the birth of her children. Her marriage may satisfy her dependency needs to some extent, but more often than not women are disappointed emotionally by marriage. The dreams of finally having someone to love and care for her are somewhat dampened. Even in a happy marriage the woman's search for equal emotional exchange, acceptance, and love falls short. A new infant can make the woman feel both pleased and proud that here is the proof that she can produce something of worth—a perfect, beautiful, healthy little baby, which came from inside her. The baby immediately becomes a symbol of her self-worth. The baby can be an extension of herself in the world.

As we know, a newborn infant does not yet have a fixed personality—it is not until approximately age two that toddlers assert themselves and fight for their sense of autonomy and independence. In those early months when the baby is developing it spends all of its time with a woman who has come to feel that her baby is her only domain in life—the only person and place over whom she has some power and control. Psychological theories always blame mothers for all of our neuroses, but that is only an indictment of a society that restricts women from developing other aspects of themselves and their lives, a society that keeps women in the home doing domestic chores and raising children. It is not mothers who are to blame. Mothers do as best as they can do in their social role. It is quite amazing that people turn out as well as they do given the level of deprivation and oppression women experience. Women are angry and depressed, they feel themselves to be empty, unworthy, and undeserving, and yet they manage to give love, care, protection, and nurturance to their infants and children.

What may begin to happen in the economy of the dependency dynamic in the couple is that the woman shifts some of her dependency onto her children and away from her partner. She becomes involved with her children emotionally in ways that may be more intimate than with her partner. The man who may have difficulty in feeling close to and relating intimately with his children is further distanced and removed from the picture. First he is not there equally because he is out at work and then when he is there he still remains an outsider. It is a vicious cycle. Children feel deprived of their father and fathers are deprived of their children.

The mother who feels deprived of emotional involvement with her partner turns her needs and attentions to her children. Her deprivation together with her social role as mother tends to make her overly involved with her children, too attached to them. We come full circle. The boy child attempts to separate himself from this woman he has been attached to by defining himself as not like her. He represses aspects of himself that he has taken in from her. He separates defensively and constructs psychological boundaries that hide his own femininity and dependency. Unconsciously he comes to feel frightened of women and their power, which he buries in his infantile memories. As a man he comes to feel frightened of women's needs for him because he fears that he will be taken over and trapped. He remembers his mother needing and holding onto him in certain ways and has difficulty in his mature attachments to a woman.

Girls, on the other hand, have a more difficult time breaking away from their mother's needs and dependency. After all, who better than a daughter to be aware of the needs of someone so close? Mother expects to be looked after by a daughter in a way that she doesn't with her son. The daughter has learned not to expect emotional caretaking (after all, mother feels deprived of it and didn't get it) and she learns that she must get it another way—by giving to others. She comes to feel hungry, deprived, and frightened of her own "insatiability" just as her mother felt. She searches for a partner who will meet her needs. She finds this person and perhaps her needs are satisfied to a certain extent. She in turn may choose to have children, and the cycle of dependency turns once again: The woman responding to the needs of her infant at the same time as she attempts to see that infant part of herself that still needs and wants nurturance in the body of her child.

Pete complained to his brother about the lack of sexual activity that he and Laura were having. His brother's wife coincidentally brought up in her conversation with Laura the topic of their sex life. Laura said that she wasn't that interested in sex these days but that it wasn't really a problem and that she thought things were fine in that department. In fact, everything wasn't really fine as far as Laura was concerned and she could no more tell her sister-in-law about it than she could tell Pete. She was upset about her own lack of interest in sex and she had bad feelings about not having an active, joyful sex life. She had always been very interested in lovemaking before her children were born. When she was breast-feeding her first child, she found that all her energy for emotional and physical contact was diverted into that new relationship. When the baby was two and the character of their involvement changed, her interest in Pete reasserted itself strongly, more strongly than they seemed to have time for. But Pete, unbeknown to Laura, was having an affair with one of his students and was insensitive to or disinterested in her sexual desires. Pete and Laura were out of synch sexually.

This change in their sexual relationship is representative of a dependency dynamic that commonly occurs when a couple have a child. During the baby's first months of life, especially where the mother is doing most of the parenting, most of mother's attention may be focused on her relationship with the baby. She and the infant live in a different world from the father. If he is scared of the baby and loath to relate actively with the

child, then the world of mother and baby appears sealed
off. Father may lose the attention of his partner as well
as be threatened by her involvement with another. Unconsciously oedipal echoes may be reevoked. As a boy
he coped with the dramatic evidence of his mother's involvement with another when he realized the importance of mother and father's relationship and became
aware, for the first time, that while mother was his first
love she had another involvement. Perhaps he, the boy,
was really an outsider. Now as father he may feel that
same sense of being pushed out, of being physically
jolted into an awareness of the threesome and the loss of
his partner's primary attention. Under such conditions,
and because socialization of the masculine role discour-
ages him from articulating to himself or his partner how
this new situation is affecting him emotionally, he may
find a temporary replacement for his partner by taking a
lover.

When Laura pressed Pete about what was happening
between them sexually, he found himself pleased by her
attention and pursuit of him. He told her how much he
missed her. He didn't mention the affair but dropped
his lover and returned to Laura. Laura felt uneasy and
guilty for having neglected Pete and they both put a lot
of energy into their relationship again. Several months
after they had resumed sleeping together regularly
again, they left their child with the grandparents and
went away together. Pete, in a particularly close moment, enjoying having Laura all to himself again,
flashed on his affair. He felt terribly guilty all of a sudden and before he knew what was happening he told
Laura about it. Although she appeared quite understanding, she immediately sank inside. She felt lousy
and betrayed. From that time on, she felt less and less
eager to make love. Each time they were physically intimate, she would remind herself of his affair and get
upset. She tried to hide this from Pete with the result
that she felt increasingly mistrustful and angry toward
him. She avoided initiating sex and without even being

aware of it, put her energy into other things.

Between the two of them, the following dynamics were at work: Pete had felt abandoned by Laura; at the same time, he had abandoned her by removing himself from her and the baby. Out of anger and a difficulty with containing his own dependency needs in the short-term, he had an affair with an eager student. When Laura showed her availability once again, he transferred his dependency needs back to her and their relationship. His fear of intimacy surfaced when they were reunited. As a protection against the closeness, guilt about his affair surfaced, and not knowing how to handle it he unconsciously used it as a wedge in their relationship. To Laura, he transmitted a threat. She heard the news of his affair as a warning not to turn her attention away from him for a moment. At a deeper level, his confession played into her own feelings of insecurity. She felt she'd been wrong to trust Pete, that she had allowed herself to be lulled into a false sense of security. She felt very hurt indeed. The other woman, and now all of Pete's female students, seemed very threatening to her. Her own fear of intimacy joined with Pete's and the affair became the reason why they weren't able to be as close as they had been. Pete's inability to cope with his dependency needs and his fear and anger (the feelings that were behind the guilt) at being abandoned by Laura, stirred up both of their fears of intimacy and close relating. They came to live with the distance. Laura was always worried that Pete would take up with someone else and that became the reason she couldn't get close. Pete was annoyed that she was withdrawn. He felt he had been honest and that showed how committed he was to her and now he was being punished. He resented her distance and was impatient with her. He wanted more sexual love and contact.

In our practice we have seen how a man may have an affair as a response to the complex changes he is experiencing in relation to his partner's pregnancy, his

dependency needs, her dependency needs, and his unconscious fantasies of the baby's dependency.

Jack and Irene have been married for four years. In
Irene's seventh month of pregnancy Jack had an affair.
It was the first sexual affair he had had since his marriage. Just before the baby was born Jack told Irene
about the affair and that he had stopped it. During the
first year of the baby's life Jack went through an emotional upheaval. Irene couldn't depend on him for
assistance for herself or the baby because Jack was
always too distressed about something in his life—work,
the car, illness, one crisis after another. Irene felt
frightened by Jack's behavior and finally insisted he see
a psychotherapist.

Vincent had his first extramarital affair when Adrian
was pregnant. He didn't know why he sought out the
encounter and felt quite disinterested in the other
woman. He slept with Jean twice. Like a dream that
comes and goes he forgot all about it. The next time he
had an affair was when Adrian was six months pregnant
with their second child. Again the affair was not a
serious event in his life. Only the day after he slept with
Rosalie did he remember that Adrian had been pregnant
the first time too. He wondered about this.

Men seeking sexual contact with another woman
when their wives are pregnant is not as uncommon as
one might wish to believe. The most common explanation of this behavior is that the wife's body is too big
and therefore she can't have sex, while the man, for
whom sex is like appetite—a natural drive, instinct—
must seek relief somewhere. Having a clearer understanding of men's dependency needs offers a different
understanding of this phenomenon.

On a conscious level Irene's pregnancy thrilled Jack.
He wanted to have children and he was tremendously
excited about the anticipated arrival of their first child.
The level of distress Jack experienced after the birth and
his subsequent therapy experience enabled him not only
to understand the "breakdown" but also to understand

why he sought a sexual affair during Irene's pregnancy. Jack unconsciously felt threatened by the arrival of his child. Suddenly he felt an interference in his attachment with Irene. Irene talked more and more about the baby as the pregnancy progressed and when she excitedly reported the baby's movements inside of her (especially as they lay in bed at night) Jack felt twinges of jealousy. She was involved with someone else in that bed—it was no longer just the two of them. The jealous feelings were too unsettling and Jack pushed them away. He tried, instead, to continue to show his excitement and delight and to share in those moments with Irene. But Irene's pregnancy rekindled unconscious infantile memories Jack had of the interrupted twosome he had with his own mother and the triangle he lived with his father and mother. Jack was an only child and so the triangle was never broken—he was either alone or in the triangle. In the first years of his marriage to Irene Jack was the happiest he had ever been in his life. He finally had someone special for himself and someone to whom he was special. The birth of their child was psychologically jolting for Jack because his dependency needs were being threatened once again—his woman was going to have another strong attachment. He felt this as a loss; he felt alone and frightened. The affair was an attempt to get someone for himself, to get reassurance. He unconsciously tried to make himself feel secure by being with a woman who was wholly available. He needed to be alone with a woman—the tension of the triangle was too upsetting. He needed reassurance. Just like dad had mother, mother had dad, now Irene had the baby and who did Jack have? His breakdown in the first year of the baby's life was Jack's regression. His continual crisis was his statement that things were not all right; that he couldn't take care of himself; that he needed to get the attention and the care that the baby was getting. Jack's dependency needs were exposed.

Vincent's affairs had different meaning. There were traces of jealousy in Vincent's feeling that the baby was getting what he had been getting. Unconsciously Vincent feared that Adrian's love and attention would *all* go to the baby and he would lose her. But the more predominant feeling for Vincent was that he felt trapped. Some of these feelings were conscious—he worried about the financial responsibilities of having a child; he was aware of feeling that having a child really meant that he was an adult and forced him to feel adult commitments. Unconsciously several things were bubbling away beneath the surface. First was the effect of Adrian's increased dependency on him. Adrian herself admitted that during her pregnancies she was very aware of her own dependency feelings. She needed Vincent to be there for her more emotionally. She needed to feel his being there and holding her, as she held the fetus inside her. (When she isn't pregnant Adrian fights these feelings in herself and doesn't show them to Vincent.) So Vincent had to give more emotionally than he was used to and unconsciously he felt depleted and resentful. Because his own child-rearing did not equip him for all this emotional caretaking he felt he was giving something above and beyond what was called for. One aspect of his sexual affair was an attempt to reestablish the balance. He wanted to be with a woman where little emotional demand was placed on him and where he could revive his depleted resources by having a woman be attentive, giving, interested. He needed to reestablish his power within himself. The second unconscious dynamic, and perhaps the more significant one, is that Vincent needed to affirm his separateness. Some of the boundaries of merger with Adrian were getting too blurred. The unborn infant represented their merger. The conscious feelings of responsibility and commitment that Vincent felt were attached to the unconscious feelings of connectedness and attachment. He felt trapped. He needed to break free of this unconscious murky attachment to a woman—he needed to experience himself in the "old" ways, as he had been before. He, like Jack, needed a woman to be available to him. Someone to whom he didn't have to give much and whom he could use to get a stronger sense of himself.

The birth of a child, then, evokes emotions in men that very often have to do with their dependency on women. A pregnant wife makes visible the ultimate dependency, which the man himself once had on a woman. There are reminders of his own infantile dependency needs, of his own attachment to his mother, at the same time there is a reminder of the mother-father-child triangle—the triangle that once in his life caused him emotional upset and readjustment.

When Rosemary was pregnant Neil withdrew from sex altogether. Rosemary was terribly upset about this as she felt particularly vulnerable and wanted to feel physically close. She imagined that he was turned off because her body was unattractive, distended, and swollen. In counseling, complicated factors emerged about Neil's relationship to the pregnancy. It made Rosemary seem awfully strong and independent in his eyes. She had this almost magical power to nourish a baby inside of her, to create new life. He felt jealous of this capacity and somewhat in awe of it. Rosemary now had something that he knew he could never have, and he felt wretched. In addition, up to that point in the relationship, he had always seen himself as the secure and loved one, and Rosemary's attention had been so distinctly focused on him that he felt important and wanted. Now not only did he feel somewhat in awe of Rosemary, but he felt a bit rejected. Her good feelings about being pregnant diverted some of the attention away from him. He was left without the constant booster he was used to, and his own negative feelings about himself seeped through. He held out sexually for two reasons. One because he wanted Rosemary to come after him; he would feel secure that he was wanted —even if he would then reject her. Secondly he felt that he would damage the baby with his penis. He knew rationally that this was ridiculous, and he wouldn't have agreed to couple therapy if he hadn't been so utterly overwhelmed by these destructive feelings.

Neil's experience hit a nerve that many men have

peeked at but have a hard time facing. Along with this dreadful fear of hurting the baby were Neil's negative and angry feelings about being pushed out by the pregnancy. Unconsciously he may have wanted to hurt the baby. Although Neil was unable to acknowledge his dependency on Rosemary, it was very strong indeed. His distance was proportional to the amount of need he had of her. He couldn't bear to think of himself as being dependent on anyone. The very idea seemed to threaten his sense of masculinity and so he retreated from that reality into its very opposite, until his needy feelings caught up with him in this scary, destructive form. During couple therapy Neil came to face his negative feelings toward the baby as well as the infantile feelings of dependency that he had been trying to get away from in himself.

The entry of children into a relationship, then, centrally touches the core of emotional dependency. As we have seen in earlier chapters, the achievement of intimate relationships is an intricate process. The potential of an intimate relationship arrives with the birth of every child. Two people developing a loving, caring relationship to their offspring and opening up themselves and their own intimate relationship to this new person are another link in the chain of human emotional experiences.

VI

❖ ❖ ❖

Friendship Between Women

Given what we have seen about emotional dependency needs and women's and men's relation to nurturance, it becomes apparent that women's relationships with one another must play important and sustaining parts in their emotional lives. Because of the way in which women are socialized and their involvement in the emotional realm, and because the mother-daughter bond (a relationship between people of feminine gender) sets the blueprint for adult relationships, relationships between women are a complex of emotional dynamics. Strikingly little attention has been paid to women's friendships. You don't find much written about it in magazines or novels. You can count on one hand the number of films that focus on a relationship between women. There are television shows in which two women are the central characters but the emphasis is always on the ways in which other people come and go in their lives, the crazy situations they get into with men or work; what goes on between them or what they get from each other is placed in the background of the plot. Most remarkably, for us,

is the absence in textbooks of psychology and teachings
of psychological development and psychotherapy of the
role that women play in one another's emotional lives.
There are texts about adolescence and the importance of
peer groups; of triangles in children's friendships; of the
critical nature of acceptance and rejection in childhood
and adolescent friendships. But nowhere in the litera-
ture (except perhaps very recently from feminist writ-
ings) is there discussion and observation about the
centrality of women's friendships or women's relationships with one another—such as sisters, aunts, grandmothers—in their emotional and psychological lives.[1]
Only now is extensive theory about the effect of mothers
in everyone's lives being developed.

It therefore seems essential to put into black and
white the blindingly obvious fact that women have
always relied on and depended on each other emotionally. Perhaps in our society today the support is less obvious than it was years ago or than it still is and was in
other cultures where women gather together and rely on
one another for childcare, getting provisions for the
family, doing laundry, etc. We see the remnants of this
in immigrant family groups and working-class families
where mothers and sisters are extremely important to
one another and where there is daily contact and involvement in the extended family life. Over the years
women have become more isolated at home, and this
may be especially true for working- and middle-class
women where the washing machine, for example, is in
the home and where large supermarkets take the place
of smaller neighborhood markets and shops. Yet even
within the isolation of so many women's day-to-day
lives they find ways of spending time with one another
and forming friendships. In work situations, whether it
be on the shop floor, coffee-break time, the lunch
break, or the office hall, women talk to one another

[1] Helene Deutsch does recognize their importance but warns us that in
the psychology of women dangers can result from close female friendships in adolescence.

about their joys and woes and their daily "mundane" experiences. It may be at the PTA or the playground, at the laundrette or during a bridge game, at a community-neighborhood association or a coffee klatch—women tell girlfriends about the problems they are having with their kids or their husbands or their mothers or their in-laws or their bosses and supervisors. Women seem to know that there is a receptive ear ready to listen and commiserate, ready to identify with their anger, disappointments, pride, and pleasure.

Joanne and Rosalie are next-door neighbors. They became friends when Rosalie and Alan moved into their two-family house in Brooklyn after they were married. Joanne had lived on the street for several years with her husband Mike. When Rosalie was moving into the house Joanne went over to introduce herself and to offer cups of coffee and a sandwich. Over the next few years they developed a friendship. They became pregnant about the same time and after they stopped working at their jobs, they began to spend more and more time together discussing how their pregnancies were going, how they each were planning for the baby to arrive, and so on. Their relationship was supportive and filled spaces in each of their lives. Their daily contact and encouragement with the growing babies provided essential support. When Mike and Alan came home from work they were unaware of how much their wives depended on and were nourished by the other.

Women's friendships are a curious social phenomenon. On the one hand they are completely obvious and assumed and yet they are also invisible. So much attention is focused on heterosexual coupling, marriage, dating, that the fact of women's relationships with one another goes largely unnoticed. We might say that the relationships themselves take on a second-class stature reflecting women's second-class position in society. We are largely unconscious of the way in which the lack of recognition of these friendships relegates them to a position of lesser importance to our emotional well-being than relationships with men.

Our mothers' women friends were as important to them as ours are to us. The difference is that we have begun to recognize the importance of these relationships and to validate them. Our mothers talked with their friends about problems in their marriages, difficulties with their children, pleasure in the achievements of their children, worries about finances, the cost of living, and so forth. But the time spent with a woman friend did not carry the weight of social approval and significance that being with a man did. It was spare time activity to pass the time while the men were at work or out together at the ball game or in the living room watching TV together or out playing poker or bowling. Time with women friends was seen as something arranged around the schedule of husbands and the times they made clear they would not be available to be with their wives. The actual importance of the women in one another's lives was no less than now but the perception of the relationships was different—it was seen as less important. We can look at these time-passing activities and see them as the refueling period, the nourishment, the discharge of tensions and anger; a communication process that recharged the battery for our mothers to go back into the home and continue to give to their children and husbands.

Ruth, Marion, Eleanor, and Jean are all women in their early sixties. They have known one another and have been friends for nearly thirty years. Their friendships began when their children were young and at school and the women got together through their children's involvement with one another. Over the many years their friendships took many forms, ranging from great closeness to some distance, with various "couples" being closer to one another than others, etc. They shared their joys, such as marriages of the children and the births of grandchildren, and their sorrows during times of personal crises. When Eleanor's husband died they were all very involved in caring for her. Throughout the years, whether it was out at lunch, at one or another's house over a cup of coffee, or during one of their numerous phone conversations, they shared details of their daily lives. As a result they were all up to date on one another's events and emotional states. They shared with one another in ways that were very different from what they shared with their husbands and families. With one another they felt a sense of equality, of camaraderie that comes from having a common experience. They didn't feel responsible for one another in the way they felt responsible for their husbands or children. They got and gave a tremendous amount to one another, and their friendships were and continue to be critical parts of the fabric of each of their lives.

The women's liberation movement in the last twelve years has legitimated women's friendships. It is only in recent years that women have been able to recognize that their relationships with other women are terribly important to them, that they are as important as their relationships with men. It is only in recent years that women have begun to see and talk about what it is they get from other women and what they get from men, the differences in these relationships, and how each is important in its own way. It is only in recent years that women have been able to spend time with their women friends and feel that it is just what they want to be doing and exactly where they want to be—and not an activity that was second best. It is a new experience and somewhat of a struggle for women to arrange dates with women friends as a priority without planning it around the schedules of their men. Women have always depended on one another for certain kinds of personal exchange and communication. In our society women's communications are often devalued and seen as chatter, while men's conversations are seen to be of great relevance. It is thought men talk of politics and ideas while women talk only about clothes, recipes, and housework.

Women's experiences and ideas are viewed as mundane. Rarely is it suggested that the limitations that men have in talking about personal matters is equally a problem or that women's ability to talk about their own lives is a strength and a social virtue. The undermining of women's communications is part and parcel of the over-all social undermining of women's friendships.

Given this new view of women's friendships, then, let's see how much women actually give to one another; how they depend on one another for emotional support and for a receptive ear; how their shared experience with children and husbands and their identifications with one another make for rich human contact and interaction. We can see ways in which sisters and mothers can be leaned on and demands and favors requested of them that women would never impose on their men. But women's relationships are not all rosy and nurturing. They are multifaceted and complex. Women are often disappointed by their friends; they often feel anger toward their women friends, which is very difficult to express; they may feel competitive with their friends or envious of them.

Freud's concept of transference in psychoanalytic theory—that is, assigning characteristics to people in one's current life that belong to people in one's earlier life, usually the parents—has much to offer in our understanding of women's friendships. Transference takes place to some extent in practically all relation-ships, and this is certainly no less true in the arena of friendships among women. In fact, it is within these relationships that women bring, perhaps, most of their transference potential into play. For there are so many parallels and nuances that exist between that first, familiar relationship with a woman—one's mother— and the later relationships a woman forms with others of her own gender. As we have seen it is quite possible for women to transfer the expectations, wants, desires, etc. they originally felt with mother onto their hus-bands, who are of a different gender, because of the man's position in the couple and the intimacy that is allowed in heterosexual couples. But women friends are likewise the recipients of one another's transferences and players for one another in the rich world of the unconscious. All of the issues we have described in earlier chapters that make up women's psychology—merger, boundaries, expectations, disappointments, betrayal, abandonment, loss, autonomy—are threads in the fabric of female friendships.

Emotional dependency needs are a part of women's friendships and may appear different from dependency needs in a sexual relationship. Usually people do not have one friend but several, and there are different degrees of intimacy in different friendships. Different things may be needed from different friends and different friends share different interests. For example, Ann and Lea always went to art galleries and photography exhibits together because they shared this interest. They had detailed and vital discussions about the art world and new works that were coming out and how they compared to other works. They never talked about their emotional lives and how they *felt* about their work of their other relationships. In that way they were actually quite shy with one another. Lea had one close friend, Mary, with whom she uncovered her deepest personal feelings, disappointments, and vulnerability.

Whereas in some ways we are "prepared" for the range of intense feelings of disappointment, jealousy, anger, and love in intimate, sexual, one-to-one relationships, we are less aware of the inevitability of these same emotions popping up in friendships. We may expect and tolerate "irrational" behavior and responses to a lover or husband and yet be surprised and uncomfortable about having these feelings toward a friend. They may seem out of place, wrong, or awkward.

Naomi and Carol shared an apartment. They were good friends. They spent many evenings at home together, cooking, telling one another about their work activities, their love affairs, and so on. Naomi was an editor at a publishing house and Carol was an actress. Carol's work was erratic. From time to time she had parts in off-off Broadway shows, showcases, and the like, but most of the time she was unemployed and going to acting and dancing classes. They each dated men, although Naomi mostly dated Josh, a man with whom she had lived several years before. They each had different friends who were in their respective work worlds and several old friends from college days. Sometimes Naomi and Carol spent time with the other's friends when they came to the apartment or they would invite the other out if they were meeting a friend and the other had nothing to do that particular evening. They had some minor fights to do with housework standards, the way phone messages were taken, and once about the way Carol felt Naomi always finished the "special" food in the house without thinking of her and what she was going to eat for dinner. But mostly they got along with one another and were supportive in their friendship.

Things changed in their relationship after a series of events. Carol was offered a part in a play. The play was successful and the actors decided to form a theater group in order to continue to perform together. Carol became more and more involved in the group. She spent several evenings a week at meetings and rehearsals. She became friendly with Jeannine, another woman in the group. When she was at home she told Naomi all about the new developments, the ins and outs of the meetings, the personalities, etc. At first Naomi listened with great interest and she offered suggestions and "gossiped" about the people with great enthusiasm. Then Naomi started to feel angry with Carol. In the evenings when Carol was out Naomi noticed all of the housework Carol didn't do. She was annoyed that Carol was hardly eating at home anymore, hardly shopping or cooking. Naomi began to go into her bedroom at night before Carol got home because she didn't want to hear all about the theater group. She was upset and angry and she didn't want to show this to Carol. Naomi often left for work in the morning before Carol was up so they started to see each other less and less. When they were together at home for the evening or part of the evening it felt tense. Naomi started to stay over at Josh's more. She complained to Josh about Carol and how she was so involved in her "thing" that it was getting impossible to live with her. Naomi was irritated and miserable. Carol was feeling angry, guilty, and confused. She felt that Naomi was passively aggressive, that she had changed and that things were not right but she didn't know why. She felt angry with Naomi for acting so "bitchy" toward her and for always complaining about the housework or about what Carol wasn't doing right. Carol felt like she was living with her mother again. She avoided Naomi as much as possible. Outside of the apartment, when she was with her other friends or with her theater group, she felt fine. Why did she have to feel so lousy when she came home?

Few women friends are able to confront one another or talk easily to one another about upsetting feelings in the friendship. It takes time to bring up the feelings and to directly talk to a friend about them, and many times women find it extremely difficult to express anger to a friend. The difficulties women have in expressing anger and the feelings of shame that can be associated with angry or critical feelings toward a friend often prevent women from tackling problems in their relationships. This was the case with Naomi and Carol. But let's take a close look and dissect what exactly was happening between them.

Naomi and Carol had become emotionally dependent on each other and yet this dependency was never openly acknowledged. Because they shared an apartment and saw a lot of each other easily, they never had to make their wish to spend time together explicit by arranging dates. Naomi was more conscious of her dependency on Josh and wouldn't have thought that Carol's activities could have affected her so. When Carol got the part in the play and became involved with the theater group Naomi felt abandoned and excluded. She felt competitive feelings toward Carol's new friend, Jeannine. She imagined that Carol and Jeannine had lots of excitement about their new relationship and that they had marvelous times together. Naomi felt boring and dull by comparison. Part of the negativity that she transmitted to Carol was, in fact, a projection of some of the feelings that she was having about herself. She felt unattractive and depressed. She felt left behind and bereft. These feelings came across as anger and unspoken criticism of the people Carol was now involved with. Naomi wasn't conscious of all of her feelings and so she could not sit down and tell Carol about them. They were a confused mass inside of her and they came out in all kinds of distorted and distressing ways. Naomi was deeply upset about her feelings of jealousy and competition toward Jeannine. She felt ashamed of these feelings. She was more "prepared" for these kinds of feelings in relation to Josh and other women, but having this reaction to a girlfriend confused and upset her even more.

On the other side of this dynamic, Carol had her own set of unconscious expectations and reactions to Naomi's upset. Carol experienced Naomi's passive anger as a hold on her. She felt constrained and undermined. She wished that Naomi could have been supportive and encouraging of her new connections with the theater group. Carol was surprised to find that she felt guilty about her activities apart from Naomi and unconsciously felt that she was betraying and abandoning her. She was upset and angry about the unspoken messages she thought she was getting not to be independent and autonomous. She was experiencing (unconsciously) transference feelings toward Naomi that were really about dynamics in her relationship with her mother. Carol felt more and more that she wanted to be away from the apartment. When she was away she felt free, when she was at home she felt constricted and depressed. She didn't want to feel Naomi's needs for her; she didn't want to be aware of Naomi's dependency because it felt like her mother's dependency. She wanted to blot it all out for fear that she would get trapped by Naomi's needs. She felt guilty and angry. She was acting toward Naomi in the same way as she acted toward her mother—that is, she ignored the need and tried to push it away. In fact, Carol's mother did have a strong attachment and need for her daughter. She was a housewife and mother who never was able to develop herself and her own potential. She lived through her children. She loved to hear about Carol's activities because they filled a gap she felt inside of her. Carol's mother had an unconscious need to hold onto Carol and not allow her to separate and be autonomous in the world. It was too frightening a proposition for her mother to be left on her own. And so Carol's reaction to Naomi's feelings of abandonment, envy, attachment was in many ways blown out of proportion to the real situation between them. She couldn't really look at the actual situation without bringing with her all of her unconscious attachments to her mother. She unconsciously felt that her autonomy and selfhood could exist only by fighting off and radically detaching herself from the woman she loved and was close to. She couldn't afford to feel her own dependency because these needs endangered her sense of self and well-being. She could not imagine maintaining the attachment, experiencing the interdependency and still being able to be separate.

Monika and Jane had been good friends for four years. They were both physiotherapists and met in graduate school during their training. They each lived with men and saw their relationship as equally as important, though different from, their sexual relationships. They spoke to each other daily, saw each other three or four times a week, and were very involved in each other's lives. They brought their men together, introduced other friends to each other, talked about politics together, and shopped together. Monika and Jane decided that working in hospitals was very draining and depressing and that they could rarely follow their work through with one patient, which they saw as terribly important to the treatment. They discussed their work extensively together and finally reached the conclusion that they should open a health spa that also offered physiotherapy services. This was a big financial plunge for them but they took the risk. They took bank loans together, got accountants, real estate brokers, health equipment and machinery purchases—all done jointly. For the first six months, although there was a lot of pressure and tension, things went smoothly. They managed to discuss all the issues, share the worries, the annoyances, and so forth. Then things started to change. Gradually Monika noticed that she was feeling annoyed by Jane. She didn't like the way Jane handled people on the telephone, she felt that Jane was very tense and bossy. Similarly Jane was angry with Monika. She felt that Monika wasn't moving fast enough and that she was not wise enough in business matters. The tension began to build under the surface because neither of them directly confronted the other with her feelings. Each day was worse for both of them. All of the things that were bothering each about the other became more and more dominant so that they were unable to enjoy and appreciate other aspects of the friendship. They began to bicker openly and the tension at the health spa was so great that it was a very stressful place for each of them to be. They stopped calling each other in the evenings, as they had always done; they stopped going out for lunch or for a chatty drink; they stopped telling each other about their loves and fights with their boyfriends. They came into work, did the work with great tension, and went home.

After several weeks of this excruciating tension between them, the summer vacation drew closer. They decided to close the spa for one month and agreed that they each needed the time away from work and each other. In the time they were apart several things happened that were to be instrumental to the solution of their difficulties. First of all, the physical separation from each other and the spa made each realize that they had been feeling swamped. They had to fight to maintain their own sense of self within what often felt like an enclosed, merged system of the threesome, as it were. Being apart allowed them to feel their own separate identities and, thus, to get back to what was felt to be "missing." These feelings, then, let them miss the other. Jane was able to think about Monika—at a distance—and therefore as her own separate self, and these thoughts allowed some positive feelings to reemerge. Similarly Monika felt herself missing Jane, and the angry feelings and criticisms she had felt previously seemed to recede into the background.

When they came back from their vacations Monika called Jane and each acknowledged that it was good to hear the other's voice and that they should get together socially before starting back at the spa. They discussed their commitments to each other, their missing each other. They cried and laughed and then had the big fight in which they each "got out" all of the pent-up grievances they had accumulated over the previous six months. Some of the grievances were defended but by and large each let the other be heard and there was some appreciation for and acceptance of angry feelings. Their own summary of the events was that they had become too merged because of their joint responsibility for the spa. There was a pattern in the grievances and that was that assumptions were being made by each about the other that had nothing to do with what the other actually felt or intended to do about a given situation. That is, each acted toward the other as if she were an extension of herself. Their fighting and irritation were an attempt to separate from the merger. They found that the same problem did not repeat itself and that they treated each other with more awareness and recognition of their separate identities after that time.

This took a commitment on each of their parts. They both took responsibility for being more aware of how they were relating to each other. They each had to face painful things in themselves about how much they each wanted things their own way at work, etc. They came to see that just as in their relationships with men, where they had to compromise and adjust to another person, so too did each have to take account of the wishes of the other and make compromises when they each felt differently about something.

Jane and Monika were able to save their friendship and build on it because they were able to sit face-to-face and declare their grievances and their feelings for each other. Their being apart for a brief period enabled them to miss each other and thereby feel the importance of the other in their lives.

Criticisms and the declaration of angry and hurt feelings are an effort that people must make in the struggle to have good relationships. In couples there is an assumption that fights and struggles must go on—that they are a part of what intimate relationships are and that, as unpleasant as they often can be, they must occur because it's only "natural" that people experience a full range of feelings in relationships. Jane and Monika were not only able to have the direct discussion, but perhaps more importantly, each was able to validate the importance of the relationship. They knew that this friendship was a central part of each of their lives—in the same way as were their relationships with the men they lived with—and therefore as uncomfortable as it may have been they forced themselves to confront the situation. They stated their need for each other and acknowledged that the loss of the friendship would be a great tragedy for each of them.

Jane and Monika's experience of assuming each was like the other can be seen in different forms in friendships. Because women are so attuned to others and because they feel less defined, more unsure of themselves, the distinctions between friends may become blurred. For example, a woman may act toward her friend in the same way as she would like her friend to act if she were in her friend's situation, although this may not reflect what the friend actually wants or needs. Joan was very distraught when her mother died. When she was with her friend Marie she was keenly aware of the way in which Marie avoided any discussion about the death. Marie, on the other hand, was also aware of not talking about the death of her friend's mother because she felt that this would be more upsetting to her. In fact it was the level of upset that it evoked in Marie that kept her from seeing her friend's need to talk about her mother and from responding appropriately to that need. When her grandmother had died in Ireland when Marie was a girl she felt extremely embarrassed, upset, and humiliated when anyone talked aloud about the death to her. When Joan's mother died Marie was operating out of unconscious behavior. She was acting toward Joan in the way she "wished" everyone would have acted toward her at the time of her grandmother's death. She felt that she was acting in Joan's interest when in fact her own unconscious need got in the way of her seeing Joan's need.

Another example of women friends acting unconsciously toward one another is the friend who can support her women friends in crisis but who is unable to positively nurture her friends toward fulfillment or autonomy. The unconscious act of keeping women in their place and the belief that women's success in the world threatens society's status quo and is something to be feared insidiously find their way even into friendships between women.

Randy was the best friend in the world when her friends were in crisis. Any kind of upset or outrage would be met by Randy with support and commiseration for the "victim." It's no surprise that Randy became a lawyer, because her psychology was one of unconsciously identifying with a victim of injustice and she had strong needs and impulses to fight back. But Randy's friend Susan spoke of this in therapy and began to notice a pattern in their relating. It seemed that every time Susan was upset Randy was right there for her, but when Susan was happy and feeling successful either in her love life or her work, Randy hardly responded to that at all. When they would talk Randy would merely acknowledge Susan's descriptions of what she felt to be really great things by saying, "Uhmm, that's great." But there was no fuel, no energy, no real enthusiasm or engagement for these experiences. Susan began to see that Randy's vitality and energy (of which there was plenty) only got stirred when something upsetting was happening to Susan or when Susan registered some sort of complaint about her situation.

In a similar fashion to Marie, Randy's unconscious was in operation with her women friends in a way that prevented her from actually seeing them and their situation. She could only relate energetically when she could unconsciously identify with the experience of her friend. In fact, Randy found it very difficult to fight for herself and placed all of her own feelings of being a victim, of anger, of acute sensitivity to injustices, of having to make right what is not right, etc., onto her relationships with others and then fought for them. Being happy with what she had achieved was impossible for Randy because unconsciously she felt that recognition of the good she had would negate her legitimate anger about the injustices she had experienced. She couldn't let go of the defense because she felt too fragile and vulnerable. It wasn't until Susan began to point some of this out to her and to say how she felt Randy related to her that Randy became at all aware of these unconscious issues. By placing her own psychology onto her friends and having one of them feed back what it felt like, Randy was able to begin to examine how this affected her own life.

As long as the relationship doesn't get sexual or pushed to the forefront society allows for women to get together in friendship. It is in women's friendships that we can see the damage and deprivation that women suffer. Even between the best of friends comparisons are made about what each has in her life, and from the unconscious feelings of deprivation and the belief that one will never get what one wants and needs, women consciously feel competitive and envious of one another. Painfully we see the ways in which women friends unconsciously attempt to hold each other down—to stay merged together in the deprivation they feel. Achievements, successes, recognitions, new boyfriends, can make friends feel left behind, abandoned. Women hate having to face those feelings. They feel ashamed for having feelings of envy or competition. They feel ashamed that when something good happens for a friend they feel bad. It's very difficult to understand why these are the feelings that come up. And yet when we analyze women's relationships with one another with an understanding of women's oppression and of the mother-daughter relationship we see that these feelings are inevitable at this time in our culture. As long as women do not feel good in themselves, whole within themselves, and substantive, and as long as they are encouraged to look to other people (especially men) to derive their place in the world, then women will feel frightened of other women's successes. They will feel less by comparison, they will feel abandoned and left behind, they will feel what is missing in their own lives. If women unconsciously hold each other in place then these feelings can remain hidden.

Alicia and Ronnie are both single women in their late twenties. They share an apartment and are good friends. Lots of their time together is spent talking about why they don't meet men, why there are no men around, how they are wanting to meet men, etc. Alicia suddenly found herself interested in two men in her graduate school class. She talked with one of them on one day and the next day she flirted with the other. That night she told Ronnie all about it. They both laughed and giggled about the possible "moves" that Alicia could now make. The next evening Ronnie told Alicia that a friend of hers at work had invited her for dinner the following Saturday night and that she had invited a friend of her husband's for Ronnie to meet. Immediately upon hearing this Alicia felt depressed, empty, blue and just miserable. In therapy Alicia said she felt terribly ashamed of these feelings. She loved Ronnie a lot and wanted her to be happy. She wanted Ronnie to meet a man, so why should she have these awful feelings of competition? It seemed that Ronnie's having a concrete date made Alicia feel that her two flirting situations were just nonsense. That nothing real existed. She wasn't able to hold onto her own excitement and anticipation about what she might have to look forward to and felt that she would *never* get what she was wanting.

Given Alicia's psychology and her unconscious certainty about being inevitably disappointed, it was too difficult for her to believe that she might get something she wanted. It would have been difficult for her to remain excited about the flirtations for very long anyway, and Ronnie's date—that is, Alicia's fantasy that Ronnie was actually getting what Alicia would not get—brought her feelings of despair immediately to the surface. Feelings of envy are very common for women. They are part and parcel of the experience of emotional deprivation. Women readily imagine that other people are getting so much more. In many cases this is true. (Women who have brothers often tell of the feelings of envy they felt when their brothers were given to in ways that they weren't.)

Differences in the lives of women friends can, therefore, be problematic. Many women find it easier to have close friends whose lives are strikingly similar to their own—whether that be professionally or domestically. For instance, dependency needs may be unevenly balanced in a friendship where one woman has an intimate, sexual relationship and the other doesn't. The woman who is on her own may have a greater need for contact and emotional exchange than the woman in a "marriage," who may be getting some of her needs satisfied by her partner. The tangle of expectation and disappointment is painful to live with as are the feelings of guilt that may be felt by the friend.

Women's feelings about their friends "having a man" when they don't used to be understood (and still is to a large extent) as the competition about having a man. The emphasis, in this way of looking at it, was on the man as the important factor, the prize so to speak. In fact, that particular triangle is much more complex and much richer. It may be that a woman envies her friend for being in a relationship with a particular man whom she likes very much. It may be that a woman envies her friend for being involved with a man—any man—no matter who he is. Seeing these feelings only in that light, however, leaves out the central dynamic of a woman feeling abandoned and at a loss because the socially valid attachment that is recognized is the tie between a man and a woman and *not* the attachment that exists between two women as friends. The connection to a man threatens women's friendships insofar as it underlines attachments. People are seen as either alone —unattached—or in a heterosexual couple. These kinds of social forms contribute to people's distress, loneliness, and feelings of isolation and being unloved. If one is not in a couple then one feels undesirable, unlovable. A woman or a man can have two or three very close friends who love her or him dearly but that will not alleviate the feelings of aloneness in a society that undervalues friendships and puts the spotlight on heterosexual couple arrangements as the only *real* loving relationships between people.

Women's "competition" for a man replays the developmental imperative for all girls—that is, the original loving attachment to mother must be broken and the girl must turn her attention to father and win his love. She learns that he is powerful and important and that one day she too, like mother, must have a man of her own. The girl's original experience of being in a "couple" with her mother is threatened when she becomes aware of mother and father's attachment and the important place he has with mother. For an adult woman, a female friend fighting with her or competing with her for a man both negates and denies the connection between the women (which is probably what hurts most) and recreates the possibility of a triangle in which one person is on the outside and excluded from a special intimacy.

Sometimes men are jealous of women's friendships. This may be because they envy the intimacy the women have and wish that they shared in the same way with a friend, or it may be that a man feels threatened by the attachment his woman has to another person and the ease women seem to have relating matters from their personal lives. He may feel aware on a subliminal level of the things the woman friend gives to his partner that he doesn't give or he may feel resentment about the intimate nature of the things his woman talks with her friend about—things that she talks to him about and which he wants to believe she tells only to him, or things that are about him, which he feels exposed and worried about. His own dependency within the relationship and his insecurities that enter the relationship on an unconscious level are transferred to his feelings about the friendships his woman has with other women.

When Michael first became involved with Arlene he knew that Beth was not only Arlene's roommate but Arlene's dearest buddy. Arlene introduced Michael to Beth by their third date and often mentioned Beth when telling Michael a story about herself. Michael didn't think too much about this because it was all familiar —other women he had dated had girlfriends who they talked about and did things with. In fact, he knew that being introduced to a close girlfriend was a good sign— it meant that the woman liked him and wanted to show him to her friend. He even felt aware of somehow having to get the approval of the girlfriend in order for things to proceed smoothly. So at first Michael was very charming and friendly to Beth. He told her jokes and stories and directed a lot of attention her way, giving her signs of inclusion when the three of them were together. He needed Beth's acceptance. A few months on in their relationship Arlene told Michael that there had been a period of time in which she was involved with women sexually. She felt that although overall it had been a good experience for her, she had come to feel that she was still primarily interested in men sexually. Michael felt a bit shocked and disturbed by this new information but felt that as a man living in the eighties this was something he should be able to handle. Michael asked Arlene several questions, one of which was whether Beth was a lover. Arlene told Michael that she wasn't and had never been. But something changed for Michael from that time onward. He watched the interaction between Beth and Arlene now through different eyes. Their closeness began to irritate him. He felt angry with Arlene when she would phone Beth to say she wouldn't be home for the night. He felt furious when Beth called Arlene at his apartment. He felt his place was being invaded and that Beth had access to Arlene at any time. He began to say little things against Beth, like pointing out different aspects of Beth's personality in a critical way. He told Arlene that he thought Beth was too attached and possessive of Arlene. He told Arlene that he felt hostility from Beth. The whole situation worsened because Arlene felt very uncomfortable about her lover being critical of her best friend; Beth began to like Michael less and less because she felt he was not very nice to her and seemed to disagree with everything she said; and Michael felt that Beth's cold shoulder toward him was a sign that she did not want him out and that she was competing with him. Beth and Arlene began to see less of each other.

Michael's difficult feelings about Arlene and Beth's

attachment only came to the forefront when he became aware of the level of attachment that Arlene was able to make with women. He knew this only when Arlene told him of her sexual relationships with women. This knowledge disturbed Michael on a very deep level. He felt shaken, threatened and angry. His changing feelings about Beth were happening on an unconscious level— that is, Michael was not aware of what his feelings about Arlene's connection to another woman or his feelings about lesbianism were. Nor was he aware of his own jealousies and the oedipal situation stirred up in him. Consciously he was aware only of feeling critical of Beth and annoyed by her behavior. He was somewhat aware of his own feelings of possessiveness and his jealousy of the friendship. He wanted to distance Beth and Arlene and he projected his own feelings of rejection, pushing away, and anger onto Beth and felt that she was acting in this way toward him, only confirming his feelings of Beth's possessiveness and attachment to Arlene. He felt her to be a rival in the situation.

Women's friendships and their dependency on one another do not take away from the intimacy in a sexual intimate relationship. On the contrary, it seems that interdependent friendships aid in the success and longevity of imtimate sexual relationships. They do so in two ways. Firstly, by diffusing some of the intensity of bringing all of one's needs to a marriage or committed sexual relationship, both in the real sense of sharing the needs and also in the transferential sense. And secondly, because women friends do often share intimately and are able to give emotional nurturance and contact, women can feel "fed" by their friends and not look only to their men for sustenance. This, in turn, brings less pressure to men in relationships. In other words, girlfriends help one another to stay in heterosexual relationships.

Daisy and Linda had been friends since high school. They were the best of friends through college and after when each of them got married. They brought their husbands together and they subsequently developed a friendship. The four of them spent a lot of time together as couples and the women continued to have lots of separate contact. After six years of marriage, during which she had a daughter, Daisy and her husband split up. It was a difficult time for her and Linda was very nurturing and caring. Daisy and her daughter, Elsa, spent lots of time at Linda's house with Linda and Jerry. Two years later Linda and her husband got divorced. In a similar fashion Daisy helped Linda get through the pain and loss. She kept her company a lot and shared with her the feelings she had during her divorce, reassuring Linda that the difficult time and the pain would end. They began to spend more and more time together because once again they were both single and had so much in common. They rented a beach house together for their summer vacation, took a winter ski trip together, and Linda cared for Elsa often so that Daisy could have some time on her own. They saw each other at least one evening a week and spoke on the phone several times in the week. They both dated and had many giggles as well as angry cries about men and sex. Then Daisy met Rhonda. They were very attracted to one another and began to have a sexual relationship. This was the first sexual relationship Daisy had had with a woman and she felt terrific excitement about this new event in her life. She felt the promise of a satisfying relationship at last and was completely enthralled by this new feeling that she didn't need to look to a man for her intimate and sexual life. Linda tried to be enthusiastic and happy for Daisy but she felt disturbed. She hated the feelings inside her because she knew that if Daisy had gotten involved with a man she would have dealt with it better. She felt jealous of the time and the intimacy between Daisy and Rhonda, but she tried as best she could to keep these feelings to herself and to act as if all was okay. At first Daisy and Linda continued to have their once-a-week dinner together. Something did not feel right between them but they each tried to carry on as if everything was fine. Then one week Linda cancelled their date and then one evening Daisy did. Their phone calls became less frequent and Daisy began to feel annoyed with Linda because she felt that when they did speak or get together Linda was depressed and ill at ease with her. Daisy talked with Rhonda about this and even though they both thought that Linda might be having problems with Daisy being a lesbian, Daisy felt that it was Linda's struggle and that there was little that she could do about it.

When Daisy's and Linda's lives were taking a similar course—that is, either they were both in other heterosexual relationships or they were both single—things worked very well between them. When Daisy became involved with Rhonda there were several significant psychological jolts brought on by the situation. First of all, Linda felt abandoned. She felt the loss of her close tie to Daisy. In addition she felt rejected, and on an unconscious level felt that there was something lacking in her that contributed to Daisy seeking this new attachment. These feelings were heightened because Daisy's new lover was a woman. While Linda could accept that a man had something else to offer to Daisy and thereby distance some of the feelings of abandonment and rejection, she could less easily do this when another women was involved. Secondly, she unconsciously was frightened by Daisy's lesbianism because it pointed up that they were different people. Unconsciously difference implied lack of connection and distance. If Daisy and Linda were really separate and so different, Linda puzzled over how they would now connect and remain attached to one another.

Daisy, on the other hand, unconsciously felt as if she had done something wrong, as if she had betrayed Linda by having this other intimate relationship with a woman. She felt guilty about having a good relationship when she knew that Linda was actually lonely and unhappy because she was not involved with anyone at that time. She felt that she had to distance herself from Linda in order to keep what she now had and wanted. Having something good in her life made her feel as if she was hurting and betraying her close friend.

Why was it that Linda and Daisy felt they could not continue to love each other and be the closest of friends? Why was it that Linda couldn't feel happy for Daisy and at the same time secure in her own attachment to Daisy? Why was it that Daisy felt guilty and sneaky about having what she wanted and that which made her happy? Why was it that Daisy's best friend had to be the person who seemed to want to prevent her from experiencing this happiness? If we look back to chapter I and remember a girl's experience with intimacy, with dependency needs being cut short and of the loss of nurturance, we find the answers. If women friends must cling to one another to fill up empty holes inside of themselves, and if women friends unconsciously act toward one another as mothers, then autonomy, separateness, and fulfillment will indeed feel threatening to one's sense of self and well-being.

There's been a new development in recent years in the arena of competition between women friends. Whereas it used to be, and still is for many people, that women looked to men in order to define who they were in the world, now women are more involved in developing themselves and their own position in society. When career opportunities were fewer for women and when it was economically possible for one adult to work to support the family, many more women were housewives and mothers and did not have paid work outside of the home. This economic dependence meant that to a large extent women's status was derived from the work of their husband—in terms of both wealth and social status. Therefore the competitive feelings among women that were based on their connection to men were far more prevalent.

We are currently observing a shift away from women's competition centering on men to women being more aware of and perhaps feeling competitive about other women's achievements. As women's social position changes and more women develop aspects of themselves that were previously denied, and as women become more confident and successful outside of the home, women's competitive feelings toward one another also take on new significance. Although ultimately we know that these feelings get in the way of women's friendships and in many ways hold women back from developing, we can't help but see these changes as a progressive step in the changing role of women. For women are now seeing one another and themselves with more definition. Women are seen as people in and of themselves, and not as people defined by who they are married to. Whether or not women will fall into competitive behaviors professionally and follow in the footsteps of men, as it were, is yet to be seen. The important struggles women face are the attempts to develop themselves and to encourage their friends in their own attempts toward self-development.

One of the major social advancements the women's liberation movement has made in these past few years has been women's attempts to support one another in these strengths. For women to encourage one another's autonomy and self-fulfillment is truly a revolutionary phenomenon. It is almost too new a phenomenon to predict the outcome, because it is one of the struggles that women are making at this very moment. Supporting a friend in getting what she needs, in helping her to be a more fulfilled, assertive, and a strong person is an act of love, which, because of women's history and psychologies, requires a very real and conscious struggle. For a woman to feel proud of her friend because she looks so beautiful or is making great strides in her work life, rather than feeling competitive and abandoned, is no minor achievement. For women to feel the possibilities in their own lives of good things to come rather than unconsciously predicting inevitable deprivation and failure is not insignificant. For women to feel that it is possible for a friend to love more than one person and to recognize the emotional dependency one has on a friend and not only a lover are of major consequence.

Women providing support and encouragement to women friends holds the possibility of repairing some of the damage and deprivation that women have internalized psychologically. Because most women in a patriarchal society come to feel less than good about themselves, it is often impossible for mothers to transmit a sense of encouragement and confidence to their daughters. This is shifting, and hopefully we will be seeing significant changes even within this next generation of girls. Our mothers had less of an opportunity of experiencing the nurturance and support for self-development and autonomy than our daughters do. Recognizing women's dependency on one another and what they are able to give to one another is a determining factor in the changing psychology of girls and women.

VII

❖ ❖ ❖

New Directions

We hope we've begun to answer the question What *do* women want? Posing this question has opened up the issue of emotional dependency in our early development and in adult life. We've seen how essential the theme of dependency is in everyday life. From our first relationship with mother through our friendships and love affairs, emotional dependency and contact are the food that nourishes us. Women and men alike need to have their dependency needs met. Knowing that one can rely on others for understanding and emotional support allows one to be confident and expressive. But for these dependency needs to be met we must change the ways we relate.

The current state of affairs vis-à-vis family life, heterosexuality, sexual politics, intimate relationships, child-rearing, and psychological development cry out for attention and change. The extent to which people experience difficulties in their intimate relationships, both with lovers and friends, tells us that things are not right. Yet some of the threads of relating *are* right because most of us know the pleasure of those moments when our relationships with friends and lovers work. We know the essentiality of people we like and love and can talk to and share experiences with. We know the wants and longings we have and the pain of disappointments and rejections. We may feel fortunate to have one or several close people we spend time with and with whom we share ourselves. We all know the importance of other people in our lives.

Some people look to their work for their primary source of gratification and commitment. Work and other activities are expressions of human life. They are achievements and celebrations of our potentialities. We are a social species—that is, we need one another to survive. Although other aspects of our lives are essential they cannot replace relationships. People depend on other people for survival. This is a fact that we rarely sit down and spend time thinking about. We not only depend on others for bits and pieces of the necessities of life, but also for social contact. We need to communicate; we need to experience ourselves in relation to others. An individual living in isolation and outside the milieu of social relations would not become a human being in the fullest sense of the term. The person might resemble a human genetically but the capacity to think, feel, communicate, and be in the world would not look anything like what we call human. Human beings live in and create their culture together.

This points out two things. Firstly, our relationships and the emotional and psychological dynamics that make up our relationships do warrant our time and attention. They are not insignificant aspects of human life. And secondly, as human beings we have the ability to change conditions of our lives that we come to understand need changing. We study history, we analyze the changes that we see and we try to understand why those particular changes came about. We learn from history and from our day-to-day lives in which new directions we need to move. We often feel lost and swamped by the

enormity of it all (and this is increasingly more the case)
but we continue to search for progressive and sane social directions. Over the last twelve years the women's
liberation movement has uncovered some areas that
need changing, and changes have been and continue to
be made. With change new forms emerge, and with
them additional stumbling blocks present themselves
and we find new ways to go beyond them. Changes, on
the scale we're talking about, seem to take a lot of time
and happen in tiny steps so often they are difficult to
pinpoint. But nothing ever stands still and our social
world is changing all the time.

This idea that social change is slow, painstaking,
essential, and potentially progressive is the frame in
which our views on dependency and intimacy rest. The
entire field of psychological development is so relatively
new, with most theory having been formulated in the
last hundred years. It is just very recently that post-
Freudian schools of psychoanalysis have turned their attention to the mother-infant relationship as the key to
personality development. With a long view of history
and human development we can't help but stress the
newness of all this knowledge.

It is only in the last decade that new ways of thinking
about the lives of women and their second-class status in
a patriarchal society have gained popular currency.
Feminism has much to offer to psychoanalytic thinking.
To understand psychological development feminism in-
sists that we must understand the social structure of
child-rearing and the psychologies of the women and
men that come out of our present family arrangements.
We can no longer merely blame mother for various
aspects of our psychologies and leave it at that. Blaming
mothers is a shorthand, a limited and restricted vision.
One might just as well blame fathers for their absence.
Both of these attitudes would miss the point. Every time
a psychologist points to mother as the problem in our
psychology, it is, in fact, an indictment of our society's
arrangement for child-rearing. Women are restricted by

their social role. If we blind ourselves to this we substitute blaming the woman for understanding.

The next step forward in psychological development theory will come from an understanding of the lives of the women who have been our mothers and who we embody in our psychologies. With that as the next step in our explorations and search for understandings it seems inevitable that the activity of child-rearing and the form of family life itself will be under evaluation. Attention and energy will be put into making progressive changes in these areas of our daily lives. These changes will aim to alleviate the imbalances that women and men experience in their psychological development. We certainly have enough information to tell us that both women and men suffer under the present constructions. As social beings we will create new ways of child-rearing.

The reality is that a social revolution concerning relations between the sexes and child-rearing practices is in process. The institution of the family is once again in flux.[1] One out of every two marriages ends in divorce; 24 percent of heads of households are women[2]—and the figure is rising; homosexuality is beginning to be an open option; and many people are deciding not to have babies. At the same time there has been a groundswell of alternative ways of living and bringing up children. Some of these have been conscious experiments, a purposeful rejection of the nuclear family mold the participants were raised in, while others have come out of force of circumstances and a breaking down of the old ways. Whatever the circumstances, as new life-style choices are forged, the people involved are engaged in a process in which their expectations, unconscious ideas,

[1] The family has been in flux for the last six hundred years. See for example Philippe Ariès, *Centuries of Childhood* (New York: Vintage Books, 1960); Elizabeth Badinter, *Mother Love* (New York: Macmillan, 1980); Edward Shorter, *The Making of the Modern Family* (New York: Basic Books, 1975).

[2] Bureau of Census as of March 1981.

prejudices, and aspirations converge in complicated ways. Psychological change is hard to come by. It needs a new structure that will allow it to flourish and an environment in which to overcome the resistances and the difficulties we encounter in ourselves. Individuals trying to raise their children outside the conventional norm, couples and new family groupings working out a lifestyle that is more expressive, suffer a double difficulty. They have to face their internal reluctance to change in a context in which they will not be receiving support from the outside, society in general. The heterosexual nuclear family is the recipient of tremendous psychological and political support in our system. In subtle and overt ways, society's members applaud that choice and undermine others, so that options are cast and lived out with difficulty. Nevertheless, that has not prevented thousands of people from experimenting with new ways of living and raising children.

We know that different methods of child-rearing can be put into practice and that mothering as we now know it is not fixed and inevitable. Mothering and fathering take place under particular conditions in a particular historical period. It wasn't always so and it won't always be so. Just forty years ago, when women's labor was required for World War II, the state instituted nursery provisions for children so that mothers would be free to work. The ideological thrust in that period was to persuade mothers that communal childcare was superior and making a contribution to America the highest service. After the war Rosie the Riveter was beamed a different ideological message: Give us back our wives and sweethearts. The nurseries were closed and women moved out of the essential productive industry into the realm of reproduction and the household. When a whole society is geared to change such as this, the possibilities seem endless and exciting. That is why we feel so positive about rethinking sexual relations and child-rearing practices from a perspective that sees the sexual politics of the situation. We also feel that the shifts and experiments occurring now point to the urgency of the situation. So many people are no longer able to live within the old structures and are seeking out new arrangements. Among the possibilities that exist today are communes, cooperatives, shared parenting by heterosexual couples, shared parenting by lesbian mothers, fathers raising children without partners, kindergarten and nursery facilities run on nonsexist lines and including male as well as female staff members.

One cannot judge these experiments in any particular way because they each have a slightly different orientation. In some of the communes there has been a desire to get away from sex-role stereotyping, in others the thrust has been toward 1960s values of support, honesty, free love, anticorporatism, and so on. In such communes, the relationship of women to child-rearing, domestic labor, and emotional life mirrors a woman's lot outside a commune. The struggles that communes face and the way in which they take up issues of sexual politics will reflect the commitment and consciousness of the members. In some communes that are dedicated to sexual equality within the commune, to childcare by all members, to cooking rosters and joint cleaning schemes, there is a resistance to sharing the emotional life of the commune. The women continue to be responsible for emotional processing and refueling. The men have not taken this up as part of their responsibility. In a spirit of antiindividualism, the emotional life of the commune is tacitly buried and emerges in a contemporary form of "women's work."

It is in smaller units that we are seeing the most dramatic changes in the last few years. Many couples who have children together are now forced by economic circumstances to think about parenting differently. Many other heterosexual and lesbian couples have decided to share the parenting, to seek out employment that makes that possible. Many women have been *deciding* to have children on their own, and many of our contemporaries are involved in intimate sexual relationships without living together. In all these arrangements, the issue of emotional dependency is on the table even if it is not squarely addressed. Each one of these challenges stirs up emotional issues in a new way and demands new responses and adaptations. The hidden dependency transactions that we have been exposing between women and men need to be understood and grappled with. For if we are to change the form in which men and women relate to one another the psychologies that we have must change. Similarly, if we wish to change our concept of sex, we need to change the support structures on which we live and the form of relations between women and men. We are at a crossroads, and our particular historical time frame calls for the engagement with certain tasks at an emotional level in order to create new social relationships.

Many of us will shy away from these tasks because they seem insurmountable or because it is hard to know where to start—and because our current psychologies predispose us to a certain negativity about change or a defensiveness that makes it hard to act. Others will avoid actively recasting the emotional-nurturing sphere, seeing it as a diversion from the broad economic revolution that needs to take place, which in its wake will usher in the equality of women, men, and children. But economic revolutions up to this point in history have not seen it as a priority to challenge the relations of the sexes at more than an economic level. Although economic changes are progressive, they are only a step in the process of equity between women and men.

What this book is addressing is an interrelated struggle that is happening right now—the challenge to the power relations between women and men. We need to uncover our prejudices, resistances, and the unconscious structures we operate out of that make change so very difficult. As we uncover these ideas we will be able to approach the present struggle more openly and seriously. For changing attitudes about ourselves and toward one another is hard and painful work; changing our behavior even more so. It requires conscious effort and a willingness to be vulnerable and exposed in ways we have not known before. Men living with feminists have felt the effects of some of these demands. Women themselves have found the need for support from other women and have met weekly in consciousness-raising groups to sort through the meaning and the effects of being raised as girls. Men have also been joining consciousness-raising groups, not in as many numbers as women and usually not groups with such a broad scope. In fact, in several men's groups, emotional issues are rarely touched on. The most interesting of the groups we have heard about center around the topic of fatherhood and its meaning in these men's lives. So that although the experiments we are talking about are taking place in individual households, there are support groups, women's groups, fathers' groups, couples' groups, and so on that are involved in processing the social revolution we are part of. This consciousness and support are important features of the struggle we are involved in, because they make *social* activities that can so easily be experienced as *individual*.

Our analysis leads us to argue that one of the tasks in front of men at this point is for them to recognize their dependency on women and to take responsibility for it, and for women to openly accept it. Through these pages we have met many men who are in flight from recognition of their dependency needs. They take comfort in the more obvious dependency of their female partners, unaware of how their dependency needs would be apparent if women showed more self-sufficiency and did not carry the dependency.

Jane and Saul were committed to struggling against this traditional scenario and tried to overcome the obstacles to intimacy that cropped up between them. They noticed that they had a tendency to live on an emotional seesaw. From time to time Jane would be blue, feel insecure and a bit at a loss. Saul would appear to be the strong one, capable of holding the stability and being secure. Then Jane would mobilize herself. Saul's self-doubts and feelings of inadequacy would surface, culminating in a fear that Jane would leave him. Having lived through these back-and-forths several times, they both tried something new. Once having uncovered the motion in the relationship they confronted a new idea. What if this was the only way their relationship worked? Perhaps they always needed to have one person be okay and the other collapsing. Perhaps this was the only way they knew how to get attention and contact. They realized that they both relied on a self-image that embodied the rescuer who was impervious and strong and who would occasionally get depressed. In other words, they were both in retreat from their vulnerable, insecure, worrying selves. If Jane was emotionally fed up, Saul could not only feel his strength in taking care of her, his relative strength was temporarily boosted by seeing her state, for into it, he unconsciously placed his distress. He divorced himself from his own worries and put them outside of himself. When Saul was feeling lousy, Jane would comfort him, feel relieved that he could also feel insecure in the relationship, and felt in good form herself. As they struggled together over this dynamic and realized that in effect they had encapsulated their needs in a package that they passed between them, they decided to try a new equilibrium. Each of them would recognize their dependency on the other, their need for the other's nurturance and care and their need for reassurance that they weren't about to be left. Saul found this hard to do. He winced at having to face his dependence on Jane when he was feeling good about himself. It made him feel weak and as though he were giving up something. Jane had an internal struggle to face in relation to Saul's exposure of this part of himself, for without realizing it she had projected onto him her need to see him as strong and invulnerable. Much as a part of her wanted him to be more open, she didn't take readily to his expression of his dependence. From the outside the emotional seesaw in Jane and

Saul's relationship might be mistaken for a kind of equality between the two of them. But the struggles with which they had to engage in coming to terms with their dependency needs were not, as we can see, symmetrical.

Jane, meanwhile, tried to stop undervaluing herself and her competence. She tried to integrate the needy part of herself with her accomplished self. When she did this she felt Saul ignored her difficulties and only related to her strengths. She felt she had to persuade him that she could be needy and competent at the same time, only half believing it herself. He didn't know exactly what that meant or how he was supposed to relate in the particulars. If she had an aggravating phone call with her mother (with whom she had a very strained relationship), he didn't know whether to ask more about it, commiserate, or discuss it. He felt helpless to make her feel better. And so he would stay silent. She would interpret his quietness as disinterest and feel abandoned. In actual fact Saul did not know what she wanted. "What *do* women want, after all?" He didn't know what it meant to provide nurturance on a day-to-day basis. When he could tell Jane this, she felt relieved and told him she wasn't needing to be rescued, she wasn't needing solutions, she was needing his understanding and attention. She told him he didn't need to have answers or interpretations, but that she would appreciate a hug and some questions. She'd like him to try and get into her shoes just for a minute to see what she was feeling and then step out of them and relate to her with tenderness and understanding.

Saul's willingness to expose his unknowingness rather than withdrawing was an example of his taking responsibility for aspects of their emotional life together. Inside he was struggling against his desire to give up and not bother to learn the skill of relating in this way. He felt he was learning a new language without quite understanding the grammar, and so he didn't know when he was doing it right or when he was doing it all wrong. Slowly, he came to be able to say things spontaneously but only after tremendous efforts.

When Jane had a report to write for work she would get very nervous. She was sure she couldn't do it and would work herself into a terrible state. She longed for Saul to do it for her because such things seemed so easy for him. She hated herself for going through these traumas every few months. Usually she did rope Saul into doing some part of it, even if it was just the opening or concluding paragraph.

This time when Jane started to get uptight as the deadline for producing the paper neared, Saul calmly reminded her that she always managed to do the papers in the end, and that they were always clear and well written. He said this to her with an attitude that conveyed a sense that she could do it. He wasn't in any way pushing her away, or taking over for her; he was recognizing her anxiety and not dismissing it, while not being overwhelmed by it himself. He was able to see both her competence and her worries. He said he would sit with her in the study while she got started; he had work to do and would be at the other end of the long desk they shared. Jane settled herself down to the report and although she would feel waves of panic rising up in her, she determined not to let them immobilize her, because as Saul had pointed out, she always did do her reports and she was not going to renege this time. She did the whole report and realized that she didn't need the odd paragraph from Saul. She had done it all herself. His help had been crucial in getting her over the first hump. With his confidence she was able to complete the task herself.

When they talked about this incident, Jane said that she felt so pleased with herself for not having gotten into a terrible state. She was still having a bit of a hard time giving up the idea that writing reports and the like was a scary experience that generated tremendous anxiety. She was used to approaching writing with incredible drama, as though her life were on the line in that activity. But on this occasion she had changed that experience. She saw that Saul had sensed her difficulty and instead of trying to push her or persuade her that she could do it, he was able to give her a confidence in herself. This was unusual on his part because in the past, when he could bear her anxiety no more, he would either get angry with her and go off or he would go over the content problems and the proposed structure of the report again and again with her. In both responses he would feel irritated, although the latter boosted his own feelings of adequacy and competence. This time, he was able to give her what *she* needed, not more and not less. He related to her as a separate and capable person. His giving to her in this way allowed her to make some changes inside herself, and they were both able to enjoy the dynamic of giving and receiving in these circumstances.

In the course of their relationship they recognized their dependency on each other and the separate needs that each of them had that they wanted related to. This created a chink in the merger between the two of them so that they were more able to see where each of them began and the other ended emotionally. They tried not to be emotional flag bearers for each other but took up instead their own issues and brought them to each other. In the course of talking about the changes in their relationship they both expressed how much more equal they felt it was now. Just as they were both sharing responsibility for the household labor, so they shared the responsibility for keeping the relationship and their needs within it afloat.

Saul had occasional twinges of discomfort and embarrassment about always trying to look at his vulnerabilities rather than coping with them in the old ways, but it was a relatively small price compared to what he felt he got out of being involved in a much more conscious and equal emotional exchange. Sometimes he would feel alienated from other men, particularly those at work who seemed so intent on bolstering their macho images and denying their vulnerabilities, but in his

men's groups he found support and comradeship. Other
men in the group discussed how hard they had found the
idea of not providing economically for their women.
Although they felt that this was outmoded, the notion
that the women they were involved with contributed to
their own support was disconcerting. For other men this
was experienced as straightforward relief. It removed
the burden of having to be the provider. For most of the
men in the group though, a variety of the following attitudes came up. "If I'm not supporting her, then I
don't exactly know what or how to give." "If she can
support herself and make as much as me then maybe
she'll be more likely to leave me." "If I don't support
her economically, it makes her much more of an equal
and I'm frightened of that." Because the group had a
commitment to work through these attitudes and it
understood the patriarchal structure that motivated sexist sentiments, the men were not afraid to speak their
minds and were able to look behind the attitudes to the
much deeper feelings they represented.

All the men in the group were able to face the fact
that they were really quite scared of women and that
deep down women's equality and separateness especially made them uneasy. In all of their relationships,
whether at work or at home, they noticed the ease with
which they would obscure that from themselves. They
did this by either mythologizing the women in one way
or another or devaluing them. The men began to face
their fear of women, especially the worry that if they
opened up they would be engulfed. They sorted through
the ideas they had acquired in their upbringing about
women "wanting everything" or "It's never enough"
or "Don't give in" and so on and began to see these as
defensive expressions learned in the male culture. They
reflected on the paradoxical attitudes they had absorbed
in relation to women; for example, how was it that the
weaker sex was potentially so very powerful? They
wondered why they were so terribly afraid of letting
their guard down to women, when that was the only

place to let their vulnerabilities show. While they most often talked about themselves in relation to work, ambition, and competition, they returned time and again to the theme of their fear and confusion about women. All of them were able to discuss the occasional irrational rage and contemptuous attitudes that surfaced in them and how these attitudes often covered up other feelings. Several of the men felt threatened by the ease with which their partners would talk openly with their girlfriends about emotional issues of one kind and another. While the buzzing conversation in the kitchen could be dismissed in one way as "just women's talk," they came to see that the dismissal itself embodies a defensive attitude predicated on envy and exclusion.

Monika's struggle with Carlo over the cooking and the dishes shows us another side of the psychological difficulties we are choosing to take on when we try to change the domestic arrangements. Carlo was a first-generation Italian-American. He had grown up in a household in which the man never entered the kitchen but awaited service. He had come a long way from that himself. He had met Monika at Columbia University, where they were both studying for their Ph.D.'s in history. He respected her a lot and had no difficulty seeing her an as intellectual equal. Although they did not live together they spent about five nights a week together at her house. He would leave a lot of his books there and the papers he was working on, and Monika found herself getting irritated by this and the fact that he didn't keep the things he left at her house in neater piles. She felt she didn't have grounds for saying very much about the situation though because she liked Carlo staying over. She did, however, notice how resentful she was that Carlo never helped out in the kitchen when she cooked. Eventually she brought this up to him in the context of a conversation they were having about feminism in the nineteenth century. She said that she thought he took her cooking for granted and wished that he could acknowledge the giving in some way. He immediately felt embarrassed and said that he would do the dishes. Monika accepted his offer but when they cleared the table at the end of the meal she noticed that Carlo picked up the scouring powder to do the dishes with. At first she thought this was funny, but then she realized that he didn't have a clue how to go about cleaning up, he had never learned it. As she put away the things in the kitchen she could catch out of the corner of her eye the novelty of his doing the dishes. Unfortunately for both of them, he was making a lousy job of it, and Monika burst in and said, "Oh, for Christ's sake, go in the other room, I'll do it." She interrupted the process of his learning how to do this household task because she couldn't give up the control and watch him doing it badly.

This incident illustrates just how difficult changes that may look so insignificant on the outside actually can be. Carlo did feel it was unmanly to wash the supper dishes, although he knew that was a ridiculous attitude. He didn't really see why Monika was making a fuss and why she couldn't take these things in her stride; after all they weren't living together and he didn't really see why he should be nagged at about his belongings or the housework. It was this attitude that he brought to the dishes and it made him approach the job unenthusiastically and without much concentration. He assumed it would be quite easy and did not understand when Monika pushed him away from the sink. For Monika, so used to doing the dishes on her own, it was hard to give way to someone else who did them badly and unwillingly. She wasn't able to contain her own feelings of needing to control when Carlo was in front of the sink, and before she knew what had happened she had intervened and played into the very dynamic that she had wanted to change. Carlo responded by proposing they eat out. He felt guilty that Monika was giving to him when she didn't want to. He had a hard time understanding that Monika liked giving to him but that she wanted the giving acknowledged. He took her request for acknowledgment as an accusation of sexism and as a warning that he shouldn't have Monika do anything for him. In reality she was very happy to cook for him as long as this did not go unrecognized.

One day Carlo decided he wanted to cook a meal at Monika's. Remembering how intrusive she had been around the dishes incident she promised herself she wouldn't intervene and try and control the whole cooking operation. She offered to be a kitchen help, cleaning the vegetables, etc., but pretty soon she realized that it made her anxious to watch him trying to cook. He only had a very approximate idea about how he was supposed to go about things and had chosen a fairly elaborate dish out of the cookbook. Monika felt her impulse to take over, but reminded herself of her promise not to interfere and went into the living room to read. She found it excruciating to imagine what was going on in the kitchen and not be involved and was shocked by just how hard it was to give up something that she knew how to do so easily. Eventually to distract herself she went out to buy flowers and wine to go with the meal.

Through these two incidents, Monika had to confront just how little she trusted Carlo to do something that was previously in her sphere of competence. Even though it wasn't an enormous issue it highlighted a dynamic that is often present between women and men. The woman feels desperately that she wants to be given to or that she wants the domestic arrangements to change, but she has become so habituated to her way of doing things or so unused to receiving that disengaging from the process and letting the other person take a new role are very hard.

Doug and Jean made a commitment to raising their child together. They had decided that the only way to break the sex-role stereotyped ideas that a child takes in would be to provide the child, from its first day, with an environment in which they participated equally. They were both university teachers and so their schedules were a lot more flexible than most. They felt they were more privileged than their friends, for they would not have to take part-time jobs and reduce their living standards in order to both be fully involved in parenting. They could approach joint parenting with extremely good conditions and they didn't really envision any problems. Before the baby arrived, they had discussed some of their fears and fantasies. Jean worried about whether the baby would think she were still special if she weren't the only present parent. Doug talked about being scared of the tininess of the baby and feeling clumsy, worrying that he would have only theories about how to stop the child's crying and not really knowing how to soothe the baby. When Jean went into labor, Doug was with her and stayed with her throughout the delivery. The experience was a totally ecstatic one for the two of them and they felt very close and happy.

When they brought the baby home from the hospital they were determined to be equally involved. They had noticed that their friends, John and Mary, who started off with the same intentions, were having a difficult time keeping to that commitment. Economic factors intervened in John and Mary's relationship when John was offered a job with a TV company and felt he couldn't turn down either the opportunity or the money. Mary found herself alone with the baby most of the time, and because she couldn't find anyone to look after the baby for the time John was meant to put in, she delayed going back to work for another few months and then eventually gave up on her part-time job altogether. John was not as eager to look after the baby when he came home, and Mary, feeling somewhat resentful of his ability to breeze in and out of childcare when he could manage it, kept the baby near to herself, thus reinforcing the sense that John had that he didn't exactly know how to relate to the child for more than a few minutes at a time.

Other friends had other versions of the same story

and seeing this around them made Doug and Jean very wary of not making the same mistakes. Jennie was born at the beginning of the long summer vacation, so they both had three months of time free of classes and formal work commitments. For the first few weeks they both seemed to spend all of their time with the baby, they were both reluctant to leave the house for very long and were caught up in the feeding, diapering environment of Jennie's needs. They both felt good about their participation and as the baby moved into its second month, one or the other of them would go off for several hours at a time, confident that the other parent would be able to interpret the meaning of the baby's various cries and gurgles.

School term came around again and Doug went off to his office to advise his students, taking Jennie with him, as he and Jean had devised a scheme for when each of them would look after the baby based on their schedules. Jean remembers watching Doug prepare Jennie for the trip, wrapping her up, taking along a bottle and various toys for her to play with, but neglecting to take diapers or the cream for diaper rash. At the moment, Jean suffered a fear that she thought had been worked through—her distrust of Doug's ability to be a good caretaker. She had felt tempted to pack up all the things that Jennie would need for the few hours but had steeled herself against doing this, telling herself that it was controlling and inconsiderate. Doug might feel insulted or undermined. Jean felt torn but they worked very hard in their relationship to not reproduce the kinds of sexist assumptions and actions that we all engage in almost automatically, and packing Jennie's things up would have implied that Doug was "helping" her out rather than shouldering his responsibility. Jean held back from her impulse to push diapers in the bag and sat with the complicated feelings stirred up in her when Doug went out the door with Jennie, underequipped.

About an hour later Doug rushed into the house to

pick up some diapers. The college was situated on a campus so the nearest place to replenish supplies was home. Later that day they talked about what happened. Doug said how angry he was with himself for not really being on top of the situation 100 percent and for the ways in which he did rely on Jean to take care of the details. Forgetting the diapers had brought up a momentary feeling that he didn't really want to be doing all this childcare. He felt able to accept the feeling in himself, not judge himself for being that way, and get a grip on the situation again. When Jean told him that she had noticed that he had left without diapers, he was at first annoyed, but when she explained what a hard internal tussle she had to leave the situation that way, he saw all the ramifications and was grateful. They both felt that they had made a significant step forward in terms of trying to be joint parents. Jean had to give up control, and Doug saw that if he wasn't alert in the detailed way he needed to be, he would be giving less than adequate care. If Jean had just stepped in and righted the situation, he would not have begun developing those skills normally associated with femininity, like attention to detail.

This struggle was one that came up in various forms through Jennie's infancy. Once when Doug was working intently on a paper with a colleague, Jennie was making a lot of noise in the other room. He was so engrossed in his work that he couldn't really tear himself away to see what Jennie was wanting. He kept giving her juice and when she cried again, more juice. When Jean came home a couple of hours later, she noticed that Jennie's diaper was really soaked. Doug hadn't put together that some of the crying was as a result of the wet diaper, caused by so much fluid. It wasn't a major disaster, but it reminded Doug of how fathering in the way he was committed to doing it was much more than a custodial role. That being available to Jennie meant that if he were working hard, he would have to take short breaks to be attentive to her. With such incidents Jean had to struggle with herself against a prejudiced notion that she knew best, that maybe she and Doug were making a mistake about all this, maybe they had gone out on a bit of a limb. These thoughts occurred only infrequently, for most of the time she was aware of the difference between her life and that of her friends. She found that Doug's participation meant that she could still be involved with things at work that interested her. Although she wasn't getting terribly much sleep these days, she felt very good in herself. She felt close to Doug and really valued the shared parenting they were doing. She loved time with Jennie and rarely felt short-tempered, and she maintained a reasonably lively interest in the outer world. She became an example to her friends who started to have children and who had been discouraged by the difficulties others in the circle committed to joint child-rearing had encountered.

When Jennie joined the daycare center at the university, the staff there commented on how little separation anxiety she seemed to exhibit in the morning and the relative ease with which she took to other adults. Jennie could approach situations with much less anxiety than some of the other children. Jennie was the recipient of the consistent attention of two parents who were more or less unambivalent about spending lots of time with her. Child-rearing was for both of them an additional joy in their lives and both of them were able to basically meet her needs without too many problems and convey a confidence that things were all right with the world. Because Jean and Doug both had other activities in their lives and because they felt supported by each other's care for Jennie, they were able to come to the nurturing situation not looking for Jennie to fill the void in their own lives or to be a representation of the parts of themselves that went unfulfilled. Jennie was very treasured, and in this sense was a vehicle for much of their love, but they also learned to establish the boundaries that are necessary for her consolidating a sense of self based on strength rather than based on a disappointment with and a flight from the early dependent period.

Within the communes, different struggles are taking place around similar issues. Some parents are having to examine their attitudes toward their children as their sole responsibility and work through the insecurity that entrusting them to other adults brings up. In many communes where children are being raised, commune members are making commitments to be stable for the first few years of a particular child's arrival so that the extended parenting that is offered is not just transitory. For it is very hard for a mother to work through her feelings of possessiveness and distrust of others' interest in her child if the membership of the circle, except for her and the child, is in a state of flux. Children raised in these circumstances would seem to have a very good chance of getting their dependency needs met when they were very young, for the structure of parenting that makes it so hard for mothers to give children the kind of care they crave is fundamentally altered. Of course the unconscious attitudes that are conveyed to children about gender and about parenting do not disappear within one generation, but the foundations for change are being laid.

We ourselves have some ideas about what things might look like in the future. There is no way to write about the ideal "healthy" future without being idealistic. In this book we have offered a description of the way dependency operates in our friendships and intimate relationships. At the risk of being idealistic, we'd like to offer a different picture—a possibility of another way of child-rearing.

Imagining the world three generations from now boggles the mind with unlimited possibilities. The structure of the world economy will no doubt be radically transformed. The anatomy of each country and society will look very different. The conventional family unit as we know it will no longer be the only acceptable form of intimate social grouping and therefore child-rearing arrangements will be varied. In order to describe a new psychology we must try to visualize the life of a new-born girl and boy and the parenting they receive. We must circumscribe our vision to set about this task. Let us, therefore, imagine a setting that is somewhat famil-iar to us—a family grouping of a woman, a man, and their children. In looking toward new directions for child-rearing a pivotal point is equal and shared parent-ing by both men and woman. As we have described throughout the book there is a severe imbalance pres-ently in the lives of women and men, with women living in the world of the family, child-rearing, and domestic life, and being underdeveloped in other areas, while men are raised to be so outer-directed and achivement-oriented that they suffer in their abilities to be emo-tionally connected, nurturing, and vulnerable. This imbalance must be changed if there is to be a change in the psychologies of the coming generations of girls and boys. A new balance must be created in which both women and men participate in the world outside of the home as well as the world inside of the home. Women and men must develop themselves in areas of work and interest. They both must become adults who feel confi-dent, substantive, emotionally integrated, and capable of expressing and receiving love and care. They both must be capable of a positive awareness of themselves, defined and with boundaries, so that they can relate to others from a position of security and self-love. We have seen in earlier chapters how psychology as it is presently constructed makes it extremely difficult, if not nearly impossible, for women and men to relate to one another in that way.

Women and men must continue to grow and develop throughout their lifetimes because of their involvements in the social world in and out of the home. There no longer will be a division made between the years of a woman's life when she is devoting herself to her children and later returning to her own life. Women no longer will feel stifled and imprisoned by living in the world of babies and feeling themselves losing the capacity for adult conversation and interests. Women no longer will fear being forty, their children grown and leaving them to an empty home—an empty life, an emptiness inside.

Men no longer will be cut off from their own off-spring. Men no longer will be forced to be out in a world of competition, only to return home for a few hours each evening. Men no longer will be strangers with a powerful mystique who enter their children's psychologies through their absence.

Let us imagine a woman and a man living together several generations from now, each having part-time work outside of the home in which they are engaged and interested. Their work schedules are arranged in such a way to give them each time with the infant, time away from the infant, time together with the infant, and time together away from the infant. The man has been raised by both his parents, and so has the woman. Through the birth of their son and then their daughter we will imagine another way of child-rearing.

A boy infant is born from his mother's womb. Throughout the pregnancy father was involved in the preparation for the coming child. Minutes after the birth both parents have access to the infant. They each cuddle him, kiss him, care for him. This couple has decided that breast feeding is the most desirable form of feeding in the early months and so they self-consciously and thoughtfully arrange for father to have contact with the infant more often through bathing, cuddling, changing of diapers, lying with and talking to his son. Milk is expressed from the breast to a bottle for the times when mother is away from the infant. The infant takes in the smell, feel, and sound of both a man and a woman equally. His father's voice and smell are as much a comfort to him as is his mother's. In the undifferentiated world of the infant both a man and a woman are inside and within his orbit. His sense of survival and utter dependency is engaged with both a man and a woman.

As he is responded to, his trust and internalized sense of care and love are associated to both a man and woman. He takes in the caring of both his father and his mother, thereby incorporating both into his new and developing psychology. As the baby grows in his first year he begins to differentiate himself from each of them and each of them from the other. There are two people who are central to his world and his sense of well-being. He embodies aspects of each of his parents' personalities. His internal sense of security is less fragile than previous generations of one-parent (mother) reared children, because all of his survival does not rest on one person. Therefore, when he experiences upset with his father, for example, because father may not respond quickly enough at any given moment, the infant is not utterly bereft or terrified. His inner world does not collapse with one parent's absence because the infant's internal world and sense of well-being rest on a third foundation. Absence of one parent will not necessarily mean loss of self. Because the infant's needs and sense of self are not bound up in one parent his internal world is not so fragile.

During his first year of life this little boy begins to experience more clearly his own boundaries and sense of self apart from his parents, his psychological separation is in relation to a man and a woman. From birth both parents have related to him as a boy, although the definitions of masculine and feminine have changed dramatically. Gender, that is, a sense of oneself as male or female, remains, but the meanings of masculinity and femininity are transformed. So, for example, being feminine includes being assertive, confident, sure of oneself; being masculine includes being vulnerable, needy, nurturant. At this early age of one, during his first steps toward psychological self-definition, the boy is encouraged to positively identify with his father. At this point the little boy embodies aspects of both parents, and as he separates he takes with him, so to speak, parts of each of them. He no longer has to define himself as *not* like his mother, his primary caretaker, in order to know himself as a boy, as did generations of boys before him. He does not have to cut off or repress so much of who he is at age one because it is feminine. He has taken in aspects of a mother who is feminine, but feminine will no longer only mean weak, fragile, soft, needy, comforter. Feminine will also mean clearly defined, nurturant, containing, strong, creative. The little boy will not have to disidentify with all that is feminine. In his developing sense of self and gender he will be able to take with him aspects of his mother while at the same time identifying with a father who is nurturant, emotionally available, reliable in his presence, and caretaking. His psychological development and separation will be a process of integration rather than splitting-off and repressing.

As he grows, the boy will not come to feel ashamed or humiliated by emotional vulnerability. He will come to feel that emotions are human, not feminine, and he will be encouraged to both express his own feelings and be aware of others. He will be learning from both of his parents (as well as from teachers, friends, books, etc.) the skills of nurturance. He will learn how to listen to others and how to respond in a caretaking manner. He will observe his father doing these things, which will all be a part of what it means to become a man.

Because he was raised by both parents he will come to have a different way of thinking about women, both consciously and unconsciously. He will no longer fear women's power or unconsciously think of them as witches or magicians. His early dependency on both a man and a woman means that as an infant he experienced both sexes in a powerful relation to himself. As he grows into a man he will not be unconsciously terrified by women who seem to have the power to control or possess him. He will not fear losing himself in a heterosexual relationship. He will not need the defenses to keep women out that men in our present day need. Because he is raised to learn caretaking skills he will have the ability to connect to others in sensitive ways and he will no longer think of women as intuitive.

Because he has a mother who has work and a place in the world in which she feels competent and productive the boy will come to be less frightened by women's needs. Not only has he developed the skills of nurturance so he feels better able to meet a woman's emotional needs, but because the woman does not look only to him and a family for self-definition there is actually less being asked of him than in present relationships. His conscious and unconscious images of women will contain respect for women, because women will be defined and active people who have an impact in the world. Because his own emotional dependency needs will be out in the open he will be able to have an appreciation for the nurturing he receives. He will value it more and it will no longer be relegated to an invisible status. Through his respect and appreciation of women his psychology will be very much different from men in previous generations whose psychology contained elements of misogyny.[2] This boy will become a man who feels himself to be an equal with women. The games he plays as a boy will not differ drastically from the games girls his age play. He will not be limited by sex-role stereotyped toys and books. As a man he will not feel his own sense of self-worth challenged by a competent woman. He will be able to have women friends as well as lovers because he will appreciate women as people He will not have to sexualize his relationships with women because he will feel more comfortable in social relationships.

He will know how to connect to women in ways other than sexual. He will have closer and more intimate friendships with other men because they will not have to hide their vulnerabilities from one another for fear of being weak and feminine. His men friends will be able

[2] See Dorothy Dinnerstein, *The Mermaid and the Minotaur* (New York: Harper & Row, Colophon, 1976).

to respond and give to him in ways that men in previous generations could only get from women. He will talk to his men and women friends about children and domestic life as well as his work and other interests. His life will not be compartmentalized into evenings and weekends for relaxation and family life at the same time as he worries about all of the financial responsibility or having to achieve a certain status because he is a man. His life will be more integrated and evenly balanced with work, family life and child-rearing, friends and activities all playing important parts.

And how would the life of a daughter being born into that family be different?

The infant girl is born of her mother's womb and, just as in the pregnancy with her brother, her father participates in the preparations for her arrival. Just after the birth both mother and father have equal access to her; holding her, kissing and cuddling with her, talking to her, changing her diapers, bathing her. She drinks from her mother's breast most of the time but the sound of her father's voice, his smell, his touch are all parts of her early world. He comforts her and attends to her. He feeds her mother's milk from a bottle. He responds to her cries and her gurgles. In her first months of life father and mother surround her and she relies on them both for her comfort and survival. During the first year of her life she internalizes aspects of both parents' personalities. She communicates with both and her sense of well-being depends on how they both are with her in her world.

During her first year she is beginning to separate psychologically. Each day she makes great strides in developing a sense of herself as separate from each of her parents. She begins to differentiate the two of them much more clearly. Her developing personality is an embodiment of the love and care of each of her parents, and aspects of her own personality will come to resemble aspects of each of their personalities. She experiences her mother coming and going just as she experiences her father going into the world and coming back again. She is witness to a woman's ability to be autonomous. As she begins to identify with mother because of their shared gender she experiences the possibilities of things to come in her own life. Each time her mother leaves and she is with father she learns two things. She learns that women can go out safely into the world and return again and she learns that men can be relied on for emotional caretaking and survival. Her father is a part of her life in his presence, rather than in his absence, as it was for generations of girls before her. The little girl can internalize both the outer-directed and the nurturing aspects of both parents. Her books and games do not have girls and women portrayed as household servants while men do the important work needed for family survival. Domestic life and creative, productive work outside of the family will be part of her world, just as they are parts of her brother's world. She is encouraged to develop her physical strengths and her curiosity about the things around her. The world outside of the home is a place she will have access to, just as her mother does. She learns skills of nurturance and domestic work because they are a part of human activity—something that all members of the family do. She does not, like generations of girls before her, learn to place her own needs second, stifle herself, and instead encourage and look after others. As a girl she experiences herself as an equal with boys and respects them in more realistic ways. She does not hold herself back when playing games with them for fear of winning and upsetting them. She does not idealize them on the one hand and feel they need to be protected on the other. She does not feel she will suffer or be punished for her strengths. Enjoying learning and doing well at school will not jeopardize her femininity. She can identify with her father in many ways and not feel that this is a betrayal of who her mother is. Both parents have things to offer her and she can use these things for her own development freely and with encouragement.

Girls growing up with both parents as nurturers and as competent people in the world have the world open to them psychologically in ways that girls in previous generations didn't. Even in the 1970s and 1980s, when the women's liberation movement made some headway and girls and women had many more opportunities available to them than their mothers had, they found that psychologically they were unprepared for these opportunities. They held themselves back for fear of betraying mother, guilt feelings, fear of success and autonomy, etc. In this new generation the girl's psychological development is such that those previous constraints are no longer present. Girls growing up with mothers who are satisfied in their active participation in the world and who are emotionally nourished and fed transmit an entirely different sense to their daughters of what it means to become a woman. The little girl born into the family we describe grows up feeling all kinds of possibilities are ahead for her. She is expected to develop herself in the fullest possible ways. She is expected to be an autonomous, capable person in the world, just like her mother. She is expected to be a sexual woman and to have pleasure in her own body. She does not feel pain and guilt about her mother's life, but pride, because her mother is more satisfied with herself.

The mother in our story transmits to her daughter that she can expect continued nurturance and that she may get that from a man or a woman in her lifetime. The daughter witnesses her parents' relationship and sees that her father is emotionally available and nurturing. She sees a shared and equal dependency between her parents and she comes to feel that expressing her own needs with a partner later in life will be perfectly normal and safe. She will be able to choose to be in an intimate relationship with a man because he may be a desirable partner—not because she must be heterosexual. She comes to develop an expectation that a man can be there for her emotionally and sexually. She is different from women in previous generations in that she experiences men's vulnerability and dependency as completely acceptable and normal and not some weakness in character. She will not come to feel somewhere deeply inside of her that men are a disappointment. She will not look to a man to fill her life because she will have a secure sense of herself; she will not be looking to a man to supply a missing piece.

Similarly because the girl has a developed sense of self as a result of receiving care and love from both parents, deprivation is not built into her psychology and she does not give to others out of the well of her unmet needs. The narcissistic aspect of women's ability to give, which we discussed in chapter I, will change. Women will have the ability and desire to give to others out of a position of completeness in their lives.

Girls will no longer experience the push-pull dynamic in their relationships with their mothers. Mothers will relate less ambivalently to their daughters because they will be feeling nurtured themselves. In turn they will not need to teach their daughters not to expect continued emotional nurturance (the push). Mothers will be getting and so they will have more to give to their daughters and will raise them to expect continued nurturance. Mothers will no longer pull their daughters to remain in a world in which mothers live restricted lives because mothers will no longer feel those restrictions. They can encourage their daughters to enter the world, to explore, to be active, to create.

As a result of both parents nurturing and raising children the psychological period of separation-individuation will be much easier and more successful than it presently is. There will be less tension and anger surrounding the infant because the pressures of childrearing will be shared. Time spent with the infant more likely will be calmer and echo feelings of contentment, because both parents will have time for other things. As it is presently, women transmit the resentment and upset they feel because of the social restrictions in their lives. With two satisfied people for the infant to relate to the atmosphere the infant lives in and internalizes will be filled with the good "food" needed for healthy psychological development. Without the push-pull dynamic and with both parents tending to and nurturing their daughters, girls will be able to develop a secure sense of self, which will enable them to psychologically separate. Boys will not have to defensively separate themselves from mother and create a false sense of security in the world while repressing an infantile part of themselves. Instead they will be able to incorporate aspects from both mother and father, thereby separating from a position of integration into their own psychology.

It will not only be at home that girls and boys will experience men and women as active in the world and nurturant. Children will be at play-schools and nurseries where men and women will be teachers. Men will feel that this is a socially useful and acceptable job for a man. Men will have been raised to relate to children, play and caretake. Because our entire conception of masculine and feminine will be altered, men nursery-school teachers will not have to live with a split in themselves that men today live with, of certain activities being feminine and therefore unacceptable for them to do. In all areas of society men and women will be in equal positions, and in a balanced relation to domestic life and productive work away from the home. Children will grow up seeing this all around them and they will be able to develop themselves in this well-rounded way.

Several generations from now there will be different family forms. Although we've described a heterosexual family we do not see the essentiality of this kind of arrangement to change the balance of emotional labor and hence the addressing of children's and adult's dependency needs. We are restricted in our vision by the society we live in, but new familial arrangements will emerge that will open up new horizons. There may be several couples with children living together and sharing domestic life and child-rearing. There may be homosexual couples—men and women—raising children together in family units or communally. The psychologies of children growing up in these different environments will differ somewhat, just as the psychologies of children today growing up with a single parent, or divorced parents, or aunts and uncles or grandmothers nearby differ from the psychology of a child growing up in a traditional nuclear family with father, mother, and siblings. The most powerful influence on any child growing up is the ideology of the society. The norm in any society affects children in every aspect of their lives outside of their home, even when their home life looks radically different from the norm. In our future projections, even if both sexes are not present in a particular household, children's models will change. Men will be in nurturing roles in other households, in nursery schools, and the like. Women will be seen in the home and the outside world. The multidimensional aspects of women and men will be visible to all and provide children with models to identify with. If, in generations to come, men and women raise boys to be nurturers and girls to develop as autonomous people out in the world, then whatever the actual form of family life—be it communal, heterosexual, homosexual, single parent—psychological development of all children will be radically different than it is today. Women and men will come to have a different sense of themselves and of one another.

If women and men raise children then dependency needs will be formed and addressed in different ways. If women can continue to expect their emotional dependency needs to be met then they will no longer feel unworthy of love and undeserving of attention. They will no longer feel insecure or be clingy people who grasp desperately onto their relationships with men and never feel they are getting what they need.

Independence will no longer be a word used to describe an emotional state of affairs. People will no longer feel that dependency signifies weakness. Dependency will be a normal, healthy part of human life.

People will no longer strive to be independent of one another, to be individualistic and competitive. People's need for one another, the need for contact and connection and emotional sharing and care and love, will be accepted as natural to human life. There will be a clearer understanding between the difference between psychological separateness—a complete and secure sense of self—and independence. It will be common knowledge that it is only through satisfaction of our dependency needs and the security of loving and nurturing relationships which provide us with an emotional anchor that we can truly feel autonomous.

Women will no longer carry the dependency in relationships. Women and men will be interdependent and each will have the ability to give nurturance and the ability to receive love and care. People's emotional interdependency will be acknowledged.

Women and men will no longer look to a partner to fill empty parts of themselves but instead will approach one another with the desire to be close to another person; to share; to experience pleasure together; to stand by one another in times of stress and pain; to offer one another support and encouragement in developing, creating, and participating fully in life.

These speculations about the future may seem farfetched and hard to achieve but experiments in living arrangements and child-rearing that are going on today have already opened up interesting possibilities for the next generation of children and adults. Women choosing to raise children on their own or with other women are beginning to not have to convey a sense of inadequacy of such an environment. Indeed the word *family* is taking on a different and broader meaning. It does not signify only a traditional nuclear family structure consisting of a present but ambivalent nurturer-mother, and a father who is there just a few minutes in the morning, a few minutes at night, and on Saturday and Sunday. The families that our children live in and internalize, and the emotional values and psychologies they are developing, are already different from the notions and images that we carry. We are involved in social revolution albeit at a minor scale. The possibilities that such developments open up should be looked at optimistically. They foretell the kinds of changes that we feel are so very urgent if the sexes are going to bridge the great divide and create a public and private world together.

BIBLIOGRAPHY

ARCANA, Judith. *Our Mothers' Daughters*: Berkeley, California, 1979.

ARIES, Philippe. *Centuries of Childhood: A Social History of Family Life*: New York, 1960.

BADINTER, Elisabeth. *Mother Love*: New York, 1980.

BAKER MILLER, Jean. *Psychoanalysis and Women*: London, 1973.

_____. *Towards a New Psychology of Women*: Boston, 1976.

BALINT, Alice. *The Early Years of Life: A Psychoanalytic Study:* New York, 1954.

BELOTTI, Elena Gianini. *Little Girls*: London, 1975.

BERNARD, Jessie. *The Future of Marriage*: New York, 1972.

_____. *The Future of Motherhood*: New York, 1974.

BOWLBY, John. *Attachment and Loss*, Volumes 1 and 2: London, 1969, 1973.

CHASSEGUET-SMIRGEL, Janine. *Female Sexuality*: Ann Arbor, 1970.

CHODOROW, Nancy. *The Reproduction of Mothering:*

Psychoanalysis and the Sociology of Gender: Berkeley, 1978.

DALY, A. *Mothers*: London, 1976.

DE BEAUVOIR, Simone. *The Second Sex*: New York, 1952.

DEUTSCH, Helene. *The Psychology of Women*, Volumes 1 and 2: New York, 1944, 1945.

DINNERSTEIN, Dorothy. *The Mermaid and the Minotaur: Sexual Arrangements and Human Malaise*: New York, 1976. Published in London, 1978, as *The Rocking of the Cradle and the Ruling of the World*.

DOWLING, Colette. *The Cinderella Complex*: New York, 1981.

EICHENBAUM, L., and Orbach, S. *Outside In . . . Inside Out & Women's Psychology: A Feminist Psychoanalytic Approach*: London, 1982. Published in expanded edition in New York, 1983, as *Understanding Women*.

FAIRBAIRN, W.R.D. *Psychoanalytic Studies of the Personality*: London, 1952.

FOUCAULT, Michel. *The History of Sexuality*, Volume 1, AW Introduction: New York, 1978.

FRIDAY, Nancy. *My Mother, My Self*: New York, 1977, London, 1979.

GILBERT, L., and Webster, P. *Bound by Love: The Sweet Trap of Daughterhood*: Boston, 1982.

GUNTRIP, Harry. *Schizoid Phenomena and Object Relations Theory*: London, 1968.

HAMMER, Signe. *Daughters and Mothers, Mothers and Daughters*: New York, 1975.

_____. *Passionate Attachments*: New York, 1982.

HITE, Shere. *The Hite Report*: New York and London, 1977.

_____. *The Hite Report on Male Sexuality*: New York, 1981.

LAZARRE, Jane. *The Mother Knot*: New York, 1976.

LEEFELOT, Christine, and Callenbach, Ernest. *The Art of Friendship*: New York, 1981.

MACCOBY, Eleanor, and Jackun, Carol. *The Psychol-*

ogy of Sex Differences: Stanford, California, 1974.

MAHLER, Margaret S., Pine, Fred, and Bergman, Anni. *The Psychological Birth of the Human Infant: Symbiosis and Individuation*: New York and London, 1975.

MASTERS, William H., and Johnson, Virginia E. *Human Sexual Response*: Boston, 1966.

MONEY, John, and Erhardt, Anke. *Man and Woman, Boy and Girl: The Differentiation and Dimorphism of Gender Identity From Conception to Maturity*: Baltimore, 1972, London, 1973.

OAKLEY, Ann. *Sex, Gender and Society*: London, 1972.

OLSEN, Paul. *Sons and Mothers: Why Men Behave as They Do*: New York, 1981.

ORBACH, Susie. *Fat Is a Feminist Issue*: London and New York, 1978.

———. *Fat Is a Feminist Issue II*: London and New York, 1982.

RICH, Adrienne. *Of Woman Born: Motherhood as Experience and Institution*: New York, 1976, London, 1977.

SCARFE, Maggie. *Unfinished Business*: New York, 1980, London, 1981.

SPITZ, Rene A. *The First Year of Life: A Psychoanalytic Study of Normal and Deviant Development of Object Relation*: New York, 1975.

STOLLER, Robert J. *Sex and Gender: On the Development of Masculinity and Femininity*: New York, 1968, London, 1969.

WINNICOTT, D. W. *The Maturational Processes and the Facilitating Environment*: London, 1963.

ZILBERGELD, Bernard. *Men and Sex*: New York, 1978, London, 1979.

INDEX

❖ ❖ ❖

Intimacy
emotional dependency
and, 92-93
emotional interchange in,
42
fear of, 54, 63-64, 79-93
insecurity and, 40
in sexual relationships,
111-13

Jealousy, 20
fantasy and, 21
felt by fathers, 149, 150
in mother-daughter rela-
tionship, 38, 46
men's of women's friend-
ships, 172-74
Johnson, Virginia E., 107,
117

Kinsey, Alfred C., 107

Lerner, Harriet, 117*n*
Lesbian couples
fear of intimacy in, 85-86
fear of merging in, 124-26
men's jealousy of, 173-74
women's friendships and,
175-77
Loss, anticipation of, 60
Love, *see* Falling in love

Macho self-image, 119-20
Mahler, Margaret S., 25*n*
*Making of the Modern
Family, The*
(Shorter), 183*n*
Marriage
clandestine love affairs
and, 36-39, 64, 90
economic basis of, 2, 10

nurturance needs in, 47-48
pressures for, 21
unsatisfactory, 29-35
See also Heterosexual
couples
Masculinity
dependence excluded from
notion of, 51
injunctions and rules
about, 13
mask of, 52
sexuality and, 112, 126-27
Masters, William H.,
107-117
Mastery, 115
Masturbation, 134
"Maternal" nurturance, 40
Men's consciousness-raising
groups, 187, 191-93
Merger
in friendships, 165-66
with mother, 84
in pregnancy, 151
psychological, 98
sexual, fear of, 120-26
*Mermaid and the Mcnotaur,
The* (Dinnerstein),
205*n*
Money, dynamics of couple
relationship and, 98
Mother-daughter relation-
ship, 13, 17
ambivalence of, 48
idealized image of, 32-33,
35
inadequate nurturance in,
25-27, 44
jealousy in, 38
pressures on, 47-48
push-pull dynamic of,
45-46, 136

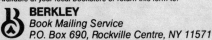

FOR TODAY'S WOMAN!

Bestsellers you've been hearing about—and want to read

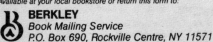